Leicestershire's Stations

An Historical Perspective

Leicestershire's Stations

An Historical Perspective

Andrew Moore

Laurel House Publishing

ISBN 0 9533628 0 9

Design & typesetting by Laburnum Graphics Ltd., Leicester.
Published by Laurel House Publishing, 8 Tennyson Street, Narborough, Leicester LE9 5FD
Printed in England

Contents

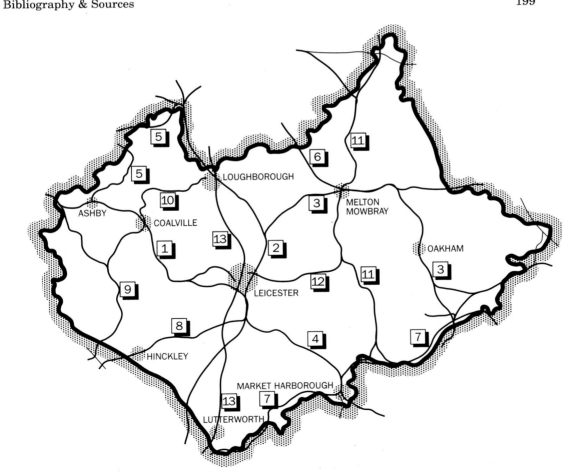

The Railways of Leicestershire indicated by Section Number

PREFACE

The earliest stations in Leicestershire were opened in 1832 on the first passenger line in the Midlands, the Leicester & Swannington Railway. Over 60 years later, the last examples (with just a few exceptions) appeared on the country's final major railway, the Great Central's London extension. During this period, the styles and fortunes of the County's stations varied tremendously, and in this volume, by recording their main aspects and features, it is intended to show this variety and explain the reasons behind the changes. The stations of Rutland are included as Rutland was merged with Leicestershire between 1974 and 1997.

It is hoped the book will be read not only by those interested in local railways, but also by people who used the stations until their widespread closure, recalling places which may have become familiar sights in the course of their travels on business or recreation.

The intention is to balance a pictorial journey with informative notes on each station so that the book may also be of assistance to railway historians – or indeed students of village or social history. With this in mind accurate dating of significant changes in a station's life has been an important aim, together with relevant opening and closing dates.

Regarding dating of closures, the normal convention has been adopted by citing the first date on which no public service was available. Also, names of stations used are those which have appeared in the various companies' Public Timetables and dates of any name changes are those officially announced by the operating company or, failing this, their first appearance in the Public Timetable.

Fortunately, many of the Midland Railway traffic figures for individual stations have survived – and a few of the LNER – and extracts have been included in an appendix which allows useful comparison of most stations at particular periods. A bibliography is also included containing details of primary and secondary sources of information, some of the volumes listed providing useful background histories to the railways in Leicestershire.

In locating information for the project, checking typescripts and for sources of photographs many people have helped. In particular I would like to thank most sincerely for their valued assistance: John Bailey, M.H.Billington, R.M.Casserley, M.A.Cooke, Sir Neil Cossons, W.F.Deebank, Dr R.Gulliver, Les Hales, Alan Johnson, Kevin Lane, Andy Lowe, Andrew Muckley, Brian Sadler, Adrian Sanderson, D.E.Shepherd, R.J. Taylor, Richard Tench, Jan Zientek and staff at the Leicestershire Record Office. Appreciation also goes to the late: M.I. Bray, J.C. Kirby, H.W. Sadler, B.J. Smith and R.E.Tustin.

(Uncredited photographs are by the author or from sources which, regrettably, cannot be traced.)

Andrew Moore   1998

Virtually from their inception, railways and their stations became so important to town and village life that at one time it would have been difficult to imagine life without them. Passenger stations and their goods yards became vital with communities relying on them for movement of themselves and their daily needs. To some degree everyone was affected, both socially and economically, at the arrival of their local lines.

In Leicestershire, although hard to imagine now, nearly every town and village was no more than a few miles from access to the railway system. Everyone had a local station (sometimes more than one) usually within reasonable walking distance. It was a place that became of great importance to each community.

Although the stations all had the same function — as a transfer point between road and rail — they were designed and developed in a variety of ways. Influencing this variety were many factors.

Of major consideration was the amount of money available and the number of people they expected to serve, so determining the overall size of the buildings, whilst the architecture depended largely on a combination of the importance the railway company placed on their stations and the period of construction.

In the very early days very simple structures were provided, mainly with booking facilities only and without even a platform or waiting shelter. Some stops on the County's first line, the Leicester & Swannington Railway (1832-3), were typical, but were considered quite sufficient at the time, especially as the line was built primarily for mineral traffic and treated passengers with only secondary importance. Things improved with the Midland Counties Railway (1840) although the standard of its stations varied tremendously from the utilisation of small, crossing gate-houses to the grand colonnaded structure at Leicester's Campbell Street station.

Following the basic designs for country stations and with the excellent prospects of the passenger business realised, stations became more impressively designed which helped promote and advertise the railway. The next two Leicestershire lines, the Midland Railway's Syston & Peterborough line (1846-8) and its Leicester & Burton branch (1849) are typical. For both these and many other lines of the period the Midland Railway (which eventually had a hand in building approximately half of the County's stations) hired renowned architects to design the buildings and, although there were sometimes common features, designs tended to be individual and imposing affairs.

Instrumental in promoting this grand image at the time was the Midland's Chairman and railway entrepreneur George Hudson, a gentleman not averse to spending lavishly. However, it did not last long for Mr Hudson grossly over-spent and became involved in irregular deals forcing him, by the end of 1849, to leave office. Restraint was shown by his successors and the Midland was not to return to its individual designs on new lines in quite the same way again.

The London & North Western Railway entered the County in 1850 with the Rugby & Stamford line but it reflected the small importance this company had started to place on station design at this time. One particular cause was the financial strains following the 'railway mania' years of 1845-7 when large amounts of money were invested in prospective railways, many of which were ill-founded and collapsed.

Restraint on railway spending generally occurred and it marked the beginning of widespread standardisation of station design to be used by nearly all companies for most country stations from then on. In Leicestershire, as well as the Midland and the LNWR, came the Great Northern, who built jointly with the LNWR (1879) and their own line to Leicester (1882). Lastly came the Great Central (1898-9).

Naturally the standard designs were cheaper to produce and although lacking prestige and individuality, they were functional and often not without their country-station charm. Many included such adornments as shapely bargeboarding on the gables and decorated valances on the awnings. It is an interesting fact that the slats which form the wooden valances had their ends profiled initially to allow the rain to drip freely from them, thus preventing early decay. Some became very ornate indeed and formed a major part of the typical British station scene. They became particularly striking when slats were painted alternately in light and dark shades forming a striped valance, a style that was in vogue with many companies at the turn of the century.

The Midland Railway had various standard building designs, most of which, in some form or another, appeared in the County. In 1857 all of the stations on their Leicester & Hitchin Railway were virtually identical except for size. Then came hipped-roof, single-storey buildings with shaped eave brackets, developed from about 1863 under the Company's Chief Engineer W.H.Barlow. From around this time the Station Master's houses tended to be built separately from the station, some of them quite large affairs reflecting the importance the occupier once held in the community.

There followed a basic theme revived from early Midland days comprising single-storey pavilions, usually in pairs, which had their ridges at right angles to the platform and these joined by a central bay with ridge parallel to the platform. Roofs were either pitched or hipped and bays occasionally added to one or both ends. This basic design was continued by Barlow's successor J.S.Crossley and lasted a long time, appearing in Leicestershire at rebuilt Syston (1867), on the Ashby & Nuneaton Joint line stations (1873), and as late as 1894 at Saxby and Edmondthorpe & Wymondham.

The Midland also standardised on wooden main structures during the 1870s. They ranged from quite simple buildings (as were the rebuilt stations at Glenfield and Ratby) to the more stylish designs at Old Dalby and Grimston, all with hipped roofs.

With all companies, only at the larger town and city stations or when special circumstances dictated, were non-standard designs considered. Such special situations were, for example, competition from other railways, as with the GN & LNW Joint Line's elaborate station at Melton, competing with the Midland, or at Redmile where the local nobility was amply catered for. Special requirements of stations when local inhabitants were not the regular users were another factor. Queniborough, Welford Road, Halts on the Charnwood Forest Line and Waltham were examples, all having peculiarities of their own.

As well as the design of building, the actual layout of the station had to be considered and this depended on several factors. The land available for instance, or the use of island or side platforms, the scale of goods facilities, terminal or through station, type of road access, and so on. Accommodation for railway personnel, particularly the Station Master, would also be considered in the plans.

With non-standard and even some standard designs, hints of many architectural periods and styles were introduced; Classical, Tudor, Italianate, Jacobean, Gothic, Georgian, or even a mixture of more than one, typical of so many buildings of the Victorian age. Most styles appeared somewhere in the County.

Similar to the trend for buildings generally in Leicestershire, the material employed for nearly all stations was brick (in the text on individual stations, therefore, this material should be assumed unless another is mentioned) although workable stone was available in Rutland and this was utilised to good effect for a number of stations in that area.

For many of the cheaper, standardised structures wood was employed. Use by the Midland has been mentioned, but the LNWR were the most prolific users employing futuristic modular components pre-fabricated at Crewe from about 1875. Approximately five years later this Company would also call upon timber 'portable' huts whenever inexpensive additional accommodation was required. These were free-standing affairs of various standard sizes with simple pitched roof and vertical boarding. Often the wooden buildings, being lighter and needing less solid foundations, were used where the stations were sited on embankments. Usually the platforms would also be of timber in these circumstances.

A combination of materials which the Victorian architects helped to make popular was glass and iron, particularly used by Joseph Paxton, designer of the Crystal Palace. As Paxton was a director of the Midland Railway it is not too surprising that this was the Company which first used the materials to produce light and airy, ridge-and-furrow type canopies, first seen in this country on the Leicester & Hitchin line at Kettering and Wellingborough. (Much of the ironwork used locally for the canopies and also bridges was produced by Richards of Leicester).

So, there were many facets to the development of the County's stations and by the time of completion of the Great Central line in 1899 most of the buildings were in full use. Just before the start of the First World War, generally regarded as the height of the railway era, the number of stations in Leicestershire had reached a total of 103.

This figure was fairly static for a period until well after the War, but then, with the competing motor-bus services starting to bite, the decline started and the inevitable closures came. In the depressive years between 1928 and 1931, 24 passenger stations were closed on five lines, mostly in the north-western quarter of the County, although all the lines concerned were built primarily for freight traffic.

During the Second World War business increased considerably, but a general lack of maintenance throughout the railway system and unfavourable Government policies after Nationalisation in 1948 did nothing to help the railways. In the early 1950s the less-used stations on other lines were also closed. A brief stable period followed but then with gathering momentum the rot set in. With road transport and car ownership rapidly increasing Dr Beeching, Chairman of British Railways, began wielding his axe and most of the remaining stations were shut. By the end of the 1960s only seven of the 103 were left.

During the running-down period the stations remaining in use became sadly neglected, typified in 1957 when much of the decorated frontage of the Great Central's Leicester station was removed and replaced by plain brickwork. At that time there was little money available for attracting custom to the railways, Government policy was to favour investment more in road transport. Bus services, especially long distance, improved and passengers did not want to walk as they used to, even half-a-mile to catch a train. The railways had become comparatively less convenient, labour-intensive, under-invested and badly marketed. In many cases, Dr Beeching's hand was unfortunately forced.

After a fairly short time the tide did turn a little. In 1970 the station at Narborough was reopened and generally an awareness was shown of attracting passengers by providing cleaner, more pleasant stations. Now long past are those grimy stations coated with layers of soot that were inherent with the steam engine.

Rebuilding and refurbishment has taken place at most of the stations remaining open, especially at Leicester where major work has been undertaken to modernise, yet retain (after bitter debate) the more elegant frontage at road level. Simple things like hanging flower baskets have also helped to improve that all-important image, although the horticulture will never reach the heights achieved at some stations, where immaculate prize-winning gardens were developed with great pride. Places such as Shepshed, Kirby Muxloe, Whetstone, Ingarsby, Glen Parva and Manton were typical and there were many more.

The lines that remain open are generally the ones that were first built, being the more important lines serving the main centres of population. The former Midland Counties and Syston & Peterborough lines remain open, although the southern part of the Midland Counties' line has been replaced by more direct routes to London and Birmingham from Wigston, avoiding the change of lines that was originally required at Rugby. Also, the Leicester & Burton line, incorporating most of the Leicester & Swannington, remains open for its main original purpose of transporting minerals.

Our present railway map is, therefore, very similar to the one of 1849. Should stations continue to come into use as has happened at Narborough and South Wigston, and with others opened, or scheduled to be opened between Loughborough, Leicester and Burton (marketed as the Ivanhoe

Line) then the map could look even more familiar. The station architecture though will surely be very different!

Since the building of the first line a total of 110 County station sites have been used on 38 of which buildings now survive. This is fewer than in most counties. Only eight of them are retained for their original use on the railway network, whilst the remainder are used for various domestic and industrial purposes and some are very much alive on preserved lines.

The fate of them all, and notes on their individual history and design are in the pages that follow.

(There are three station sites which fall just within the Leicestershire border but on separate lines predominantly outside the County. Their story really belongs, therefore, with those lines rather than in this book. They were all formerly owned by the Great Northern and namely: Essendine, on the East Coast main line; Ryhall & Belmisthorpe, on the Stamford & Essendine Railway; and Bottesford – which is still open – on the Nottingham to Grantham line.)

Ryhall & Belmisthorpe station in 1959. This was the only intermediate station on the Stamford & Essendine Railway.
(Les Hales)

A short section of the East Coast Main Line runs just within Rutland. On it was situated Essendine station taken here in 1958 looking south.
(B. J. Smith)

Bottesford Station. The building has been greatly reduced in size since this picture was taken in 1969.
(John Bailey)

LEICESTER & SWANNINGTON RAILWAY
AND LEICESTER & BURTON BRANCH (MR)

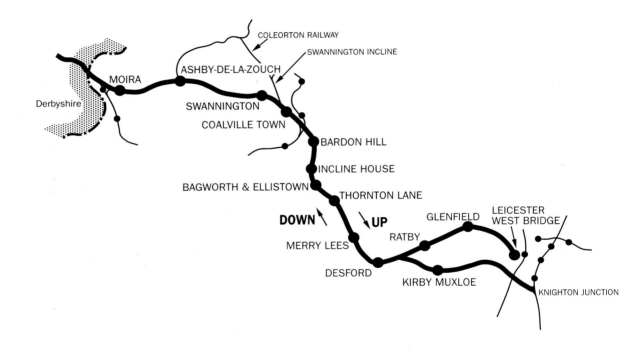

LEICESTER & SWANNINGTON RAILWAY AND LEICESTER & BURTON BRANCH (MR)

A major part of these railways is common (from Desford to Coalville) and so for convenience, both lines appear together in this section. They were both opened in piecemeal fashion.

The first stretch of the Leicester & Swannington was officially opened on 17 July 1832 when special trains ran for passengers from Leicester (West Bridge) to Bagworth, although coal and granite wagons were attached to the trains for the return journey. This was the reverse of the normal services when the wagons used for passengers were attached to the more important mineral trains.

Regular trains started the next day to a temporary stopping place at Staunton Road (later Stanton Road) one mile past the top of the Bagworth Incline. This lasted until the section to Ashby Road (Bardon Hill) station was opened by 1 February 1833 for goods and 23 February for passengers. Long Lane (Coalville) was reached on the following 27 April for all traffic.

The initial working of the last section of line – for the hauling of coal wagons from Swannington up the famous incline – is recorded as approximately 25 November 1833. However, Clement Stretton, in his 'Railways of Leicestershire', quotes official railway notices to the effect that the earliest use was by horse-drawn wagons for transporting passengers from Swannington village up the steep 1 in 17 incline to Long Lane where the wagons were attached to the Leicester market trains. During the journey wagons allegedly stopped to pick up passengers at Spring Lane crossing at the top of the incline and at Mantle Lane (Coalville).

According to the notices this service started the same day in April as the Ashby Road to Long Lane section, although it is unfortunate that to substantiate the information, none of the notices can be found in the contemporary press. If it ever ran at all, the service presumably continued only until the November opening of the rope-operated incline. (Hauling of passenger wagons up the incline was quite feasible by horse. In later years whenever there were problems with the incline's steam-driven machinery horses were used to pull up the coal-laden wagons.)

Also, these would not have been the only passenger vehicles to travel on the incline. Again according to Stretton, carriages have traversed the incline during special trips en route from Leicester to places 'as far as Breedon Hill' via the connecting Coleorton Railway.

This last-mentioned line, independently built at the bottom of the Swannington Incline for minerals only in 1833, also had a carriage run over its short route when the owner, Sir George Beaumont, inspected his property and departed from a small platform next to his mining company's offices.

The single line Leicester & Swannington was taken over officially on 27 July 1846 by the Midland Railway who were to build a through route from Knighton Junction to Burton by utilising the Desford to Coalville section of the Leicester & Swannington. This section was made double-track as a result and the stations rebuilt, the modifications coming into effect on 27 March 1848. Coalville to Burton was open on 2 October 1848 (goods) and 1 March 1849 (passengers), allowing a service to operate between Leicester West Bridge and Burton for 5 months until the southern section, Knighton Junction to Desford, and hence the through route, was opened on 1 August 1849 for passengers although 'shortly earlier' for goods.

The Leicester & Swannington theme for station buildings on their line appeared to be to rent a room at a local inn or hotel if available, otherwise a simple brick building would suffice. Rented accommodation was used for four of the nine stations proper; at Ratby (though not initially), Thornton, Ashby Road and Long Lane. In contrast, with the appreciation of station requirements improved, those on the rebuilt section and Burton extension were well designed and quite substantial. Unfortunately, it is uncertain who was responsible for the design, but the Leicester architect William Parsons has been attributed with at least Moira, Coalville and Merry Lees, each of which had certain similarities, especially the distinctive windows.

Regarding passenger bookings, reference to figures in the appendix show that in Midland days the line's passenger traffic increased steadily over the years, including the last period, 1920-2. However, during this last three years, although the 1920 figures were very high (not shown separately in the appendix), there was a sudden and dramatic downturn in business during 1921-2. This was due initially to a three month strike followed by a massive increase in unemployment, especially in the line's main industry of mining,

proposed station site was used for dumping soil from the main line widening at Knighton Tunnel.

The three halts were all proposed in the vicinity of Hinckley Road in Leicester. The first was in 1927 to serve the new Braunstone housing estate, but probably buses were seen to be more convenient. The second was to serve Leicester's Municipal Aerodrome, opened at Braunstone Frith in 1935, but the halt never materialised because of the aerodrome's diversion to military use during the war. The last unsuccessful plan was for a halt to serve employees of a newly-built British Thomson-Houston (later GEC/Marconi) factory in 1957.

Temporary platforms were used for the popular British Rail open days regularly held at Mantle Lane, Coalville. This one was taken in 1985.

such that the average number of passengers booked at all stations was 39% lower in 1922 than 1920.

Traffic on the Leicester-Burton line did eventually improve, but not on the West Bridge to Desford Junction section where, with much competition from buses at this time, passenger services ceased from 24 September 1928. The branch survived for goods much longer, however, until 4 April 1966. On the Burton line all passenger services, although quite heavily used at the time, were withdrawn from 7 September 1964, but minerals are still moved.

A station and three halts were planned on the southern section of the line but never built. The station, to have been known as Aylestone, was proposed for a site near to where the line crosses Aylestone Road to serve the new gas works and associated housing. Plans were drawn and passed by 1882 but building was continually deferred. The idea was finally abandoned in 1892 when the

Mention must also be made of a temporary platform that was used during the 1970s and 1980s at Mantle Lane, Coalville for British Rail open days, when a timetabled shuttle service was run from Leicester and other Midlands stations:

LEICESTER WEST BRIDGE

The first station on the site was a plain, rectangular structure of two storeys, situated just a few yards from the Grand Union Canal. It was built primarily for the Leicester and Swannington Company offices with the board room on the first floor and was still being hurriedly built a week after the line was opened. It contained a booking office, where the line's famous octagonal brass tickets were issued, but there was no passenger accommodation in the building until 1840. Passengers had to wait even longer for a platform, provided in 1876 and extended in 1887.

A feature throughout the life of the station was a large bell hung from the pitched roof. It may well have been rung in the early days to announce

*An engraving of the
original West Bridge Station.*

train departures, a system common on many other railways.

Originally known as just Leicester, the suffix West Bridge appeared in timetables for the first time when trains ran through from here to Burton in March 1849.

However, because the site of the building did not meet with new Railway Regulations due to restricted access across coal yards, a replacement single-storey station, basically of two, pitched-roof bays at right-angles, was built at the head of a short branch. It was about 150 yards west of the first station, with improved access from King Richards Road. A single platform was provided on which was a plain set of brick waiting rooms.

The new station, which opened on 13 March 1893, was known as King Richards Road, and listed thus in locally-published timetables for about 15 years. It was never called this officially by the Midland Railway, however – only Leicester West Bridge. For the Station Master's accommodation properties were rented locally.

Closure came with the branch passenger service in 1928, and the buildings of both stations continued in use as a variety of goods yard offices. All were removed though, when this large area was cleared

*The first West Bridge station
taken in 1893, its final year of
passenger use.*

*The resited station at West Bridge
showing platform building and the
rear of the booking office on the left.*

The original station building from the south at Glenfield crossing taken in 1948. (R.E. Tustin)

for industrial and recreational development in the early 1970s.

A footpath now runs through the site, at the side of which has been built a short platform complete with section of track, a signal and West Bridge nameboard. It is a pleasant reminder of what was the first passenger station to be used in the Midlands.

GLENFIELD

Built by a level crossing on the north side of the village, the original station building combined the crossing-keeper's house and booking office. It was very similar to a turnpike toll house, with one side bowed to allow viewing up and down the line from its two storeys. Virtually square in plan, it was hip-roofed, and for most of its life the walls were rendered.

There was no platform until 1875 when one was provided on the opposite (east) side of the road on

which was built a new booking office and waiting room, with further buildings added the following year. The main structure was an early version of one of the Midland Railway's standard wooden designs with horizontal boarding and slated hipped roof overhanging on three sides and with decorated valance. Doors and windows were round-headed on this version. There was also a small brick store for goods located on the platform dating from 1887.

Revenue from passengers was always very low as can be seen from the figures in the appendix – the average receipts per journey amounting to less than 6d (2½ pence) including allowance for journeys with season tickets. Most journeys, no doubt, were for the short trip to Leicester.

Sadly, although the distinctive first station survived until 1966, in reasonable condition, it was demolished to allow for road widening. The second station, kept in use as goods offices till 1965, has

A postcard view of the 1875 wooden building at Glenfield and the western portal of Glenfield tunnel.

A general view of Glenfield in 1964. New houses have since spread over the whole area. (B.J.Smith)

also disappeared, but is now depicted on a large brass plaque mounted on a pseudo buffer stop to record the station site. The plaque, which can be seen facing the main road, was provided by the builders of a housing estate which now covers the area east of the crossing.

RATBY

Although built next to a level crossing like Glenfield, there was strangely no company building erected here when the line opened, nor was there an inn which could be utilised. What was used instead for the first few months is difficult to assess, but we know that J. Freeman had built a single-storey house for his crossing-keeper's duties which may have had booking facilities, and that by 1834 the Railway Inn had been built. This was adjoining the crossing-keeper's house and at some stage would most probably have been used for station purposes. It was owned by D. Marvin who had been urged by the company to build a goods

wharf on the opposite side of the line where there was a small building which also could have been used for booking. We know that the innkeeper was also the Station Master in the 1860s.

Both inn and bow-fronted crossing house can still be seen east of the former level crossing on the south side of the village, although gone since the late 1960s is a replacement station that was erected west of the crossing. On this side a single platform was provided initially with a wooden booking office of virtually the same neat design as that at Glenfield. It was erected earlier than Glenfield, however, in 1873, with further platform buildings completed in 1876 and the platform extended in 1887.

The station then remained virtually unchanged until closure in 1928, although the goods business continued until 1954. Passengers did return briefly to the platforms in 1951, when the local

Similar to Glenfield was the building at Ratby viewed here from the south in 1955. (Les Hales)

17

A freight train from West Bridge passing Ratby in 1962. The Railway Inn, where booking was probably carried out in the early days, can be seen.

Wolsey factory organised a trip from the derelict station to the Festival of Britain (combined with a shoe manufacturer's outing from Glenfield station) and a similar trip to the Coronation in 1953. A waste-paper merchant now occupies this station site.

DESFORD

When the line opened the only available building suitable for a booking office was a small coal office built by local landowner Henry Chamberlain who also ran the wharf. It eventually became the weighbridge office and stood on the drive to the goods yard, south-east of the level crossing on the Desford to Newtown Unthank road. It was demolished in about 1939 still retaining the builder's iron plate over the doorway inscribed 'HC 1832'.

This building was used as a temporary measure until the end of 1833 when the company erected its own office to the north-east of the crossing. Few details of this are known as it lasted only

The weighbridge office at Desford originally used as the booking office.

The extension to the Station Master's house can be seen on this early view of Desford.

Desford in 1962. The building remains virtually unchanged today except for removal of the section near the road.
(H. C. Casserley)

until Desford's first signal box was built on the same site in 1869. It measured approximately 18ft x 10ft and was most probably a simple, single-storey building of brick. For about the first nine months the station was known as Desford Lane.

When the Midland Railway doubled the track in 1848 they built a new station on the opposite side of the crossing with a two-storey Station Master's house adjoining the single-storey station offices. There was a slight Tudor effect in the design with stone quoins on the windows, tall twisted chimneys and stone-capped, raised gables being the dominant features. Incorporated in the new platforms were stone sleepers from the Leicester & Swannington Railway as they also were at Kirby Muxloe, Swannington and probably others on the line.

A small waiting shed was erected on the Up platform in 1857 and an extra waiting room added to the main building in 1862. In 1875 both platforms were lengthened westward and the Up one raised. On the Down side though, the height of the extended end only was increased as it was not practical to raise the section in front of the main buildings because of obstructing doorways etc. This gave the platform a very unusual split level appearance which lasted until closure. In 1904 there were enlargements to both storeys on the west side of the Station Master's house and a much larger waiting shelter provided on the opposite platform.

The station was closed with the line's passenger service in 1964 and shortly after a section at the eastern end of the main building was removed for road widening. The remainder of the Down-side buildings survive for domestic use.

MERRY LEES

The amazing thing here is that there was ever a station at all as the only possible users during its brief life were the inhabitants of a few scattered

The first station at Merrylees still in use residentially in 1952.
(National Railway Museum)

Diminutive but with some style was the second station at Merrylees which saw only 16 years passenger service.

farm houses. It is not known where the few passengers would have booked in the early days as there was no station building until the provision of a crossing-keeper's house – with booking facilities – in 1839.

This was situated to the north east of a road crossing in the centre of the hamlet and was a plain, two-storey building with hipped roof and no eaves. It lasted as a booking office until 1848 and continued as a railway cottage, occupied until demolished in the 1960s. When the line was doubled the second line passed uncomfortably close to it (within four feet) but fortunately there was no door on the track-side!

With the track doubling, the crossing was replaced by a bridge and a new booking office erected, first used on 27 March 1848. The building was south-west of the new bridge, very small and with a short platform. It was single-storey, and very stylish with stone-capped gables and openings of the four-centred design with matching drip-stones. Even the windows were diamond-latticed.

But it was little used, the last annual receipts amounting to only £16, and with the local population remaining low the station was closed from 1 March 1871. This tiny building was then probably used as a store or office serving a public goods siding that was opened in 1875. The building lasted, quite derelict for at least its final ten years, before demolition around 1941.

THORNTON LANE

The railway crossed the lane between Thornton and Bagworth on the level, where, on the south side facing the line, stood a former inn, the Stag and Castle – conveniently situated for the company to rent a room for the station office.

It was first used for the Saturday train to Leicester on 21 July 1832 following the line opening to Bagworth and open only for Saturday and

Taken in 1991 the former Stag & Castle inn which was used as a booking office at Thornton Lane.

midweek market-day services, one train in each direction. These few trains were little used, however, and the station closed from 31 December 1841. Early public notices called the stopping place Thornton Lane, although just Thornton appeared in timetables.

It was officially Thornton Lane though, after the Midland Railway gave approval on 30 July 1850 for the station to reopen following several requests from local residents. By this time the double-track Bagworth deviation had been completed with the new line running on an embankment in front of the former inn. A railway office was provided at the side of the building and steps built up the embankment to the platforms which were crudely constructed from old sleepers.

These were quite sufficient for the service of just one train each way, Saturdays only – but even this did not last long, with final closure of the station from 1 October 1865. The inn building has survived with little alteration and remains occupied.

BAGWORTH & ELLISTOWN

The first station, named just Bagworth, was only about ¼ mile from Thornton and situated near the foot of Bagworth incline – on the south side of the line. Strangely, from Bagworth village it was only accessible by footpath. There was originally just a railway office, but a shelter was added for passengers in 1841. Details of the buildings are not known, but were probably small, single-story structures, nothing of which survived after 1886.

This station was replaced by a second which came into use with the opening of the incline deviation on 27 March 1848 and was more conveniently situated at the northern end of the village. This grand new building was almost identical to Desford with the same Tudor effect in the design of the two-storey dwelling and single-storey offices, although the layout of the building differed. The only known addition to this building was an extra waiting room in 1860.

The Down platform was lengthened in 1861, although it was removed when the layout of the lines was radically changed in 1882-3. This resulted in a colliery line running between the station building and a rebuilt Down platform, with a new metal footbridge then providing access to both platforms. The Up one was given a new brick shelter at the same time. In October 1894 the station name was changed to Bagworth and Ellistown, and in 1911 a small waiting shed added to the Down platform.

Unfortunately, mining subsidence, so prevalent in the area, caused the station area to sink considerably. The tracks were continually raised to keep a constant level, so much so that eventually the tracks reached the height of the station windows! Platforms had to be constantly raised also, and the final method employed was by building new wooden decks above the platforms. The brick, Up-side shelter also had to be replaced by one of timber.

In addition, subsidence made parts of the main building unsafe and unusable by the public. An-

The extent of raising the track due to subsidence can be seen in this 1959 view of the abandoned main building at Bagworth & Ellistown. The trackbed is at windowsill level. (M. A. Cooke)

A DMU from Leicester enters the make-shift wooden platforms at Bagworth & Ellistown. Both contrasting platform shelters have been transferred from other stations. (W. A. Camwell)

The temporary booking office in an ex MR clerestory coach and new building under construction at Bagworth & Ellistown in 1959. (M. A. Cooke)

old carriage body standing near the station for use as a railwaymen's mess room was, therefore, converted into a rather ramshackle booking office in about 1950 and used until a new, single-storey building containing booking office and waiting rooms was provided in 1959. This was a modern, wood and glass structure with flat roof, quite unimposing, which subsidence could not damage too expensively.

It was little used, however, as the station closed with the line's passenger service in 1964. The building survives, now much extended for industrial use, and sits alongside the only other remnant of the station, the main section of the 1883 footbridge, which is part of a public footpath.

In Midland days at least, the station was particularly well used, and, as shown in the appendix by the number of season tickets purchased, was patronised by a large number of commuters.

INCLINE HOUSE

Although only a temporary stopping point and not a place where seats could be booked, the house was entered for a short time in some public timetables and could, therefore, be termed a station. It was situated at the top of the line's rope-operated

"DEPARTURE FROM LEICESTER.

Distance. Miles.		a.m.	a.m.	p.m.	Saturdays and Fair Days only. p.m.
0	Leicester	6-0	11-0	*4-0	5-0
2¾	Glenfield	6-20	11-20	4-20	5-20
4½	Ratby	6-27	11-27	4-27	5-27
6⅝	Desford	6-35	11-35	4-35	5-35
8⅛	Merry-lees ..	6-45	11-45	4-45	5-45
10	Bagworth	6-50	11-50	4-50	5-50
10¾	Incline House.	7-0	12-0	5-0	6-0
13⅛	Ashby Road ..	7-7	12-7	5-7	6-7
14½	Long Lane ...	7-15	12-15	5-15	6-15

*The 4 o'clock train leaves at 5 on Saturdays and Fair Days.

"DEPARTURE FROM LONG LANE.

Distance. Miles.		a.m.	a.m.	p.m.	Saturdays and Fair Days only. p.m.
0	Long Lane ..	6-30	11-30	*4-30	5-30
1⅜	Ashby Road..	6-40	11-40	4-40	5-40
3¾	Incline House.	6-50	11-50	4-50	5-50
4½	Bagworth	7-10	12-10	5-10	6-10
6⅜	Merry-lees ..	7-15	12-15	5-15	6-15
7⅞	Desford	7-25	12-25	5-25	6-25
10	Ratby	7-33	12-33	5-33	6-33
11¾	Glenfield	7-40	12-40	5-40	6-40
14½	Leicester	8-0	1-0	6-0	7-0

*The 4-30 o'clock train leaves at 5-30 on Saturdays and Fair Days.

The Incline House was for a short time included in the timetable.

The incline-keeper's house in 1958
(H. W. Sadler)

incline on the eastern side (approachable from Park Lane Bagworth) and built to house the incline-keeper. Passengers were probably able to board and alight here as the passenger wagons would be temporarily stopped while they were attached to or detached from the incline rope.

It was first used as a station when the Leicester & Swannington line went as far as Staunton Road on 21 July 1832 and according to reports by Stretton was still used by 27 April 1833, but for how much longer is not known.

The house was of the toll-house type, virtually identical to the one at Glenfield and occupied until the late 1960s. Tragically it gradually fell into complete ruin despite being a Grade II listed building. For various bureaucratic reasons, dispute over ownership and mining subsidence, listing did not maintain its survival – a great shame as it was the last remaining structure of the Leicester & Swannington and would have been the oldest railway building in Leicestershire – in fact one of the oldest anywhere.

BARDON HILL

The line crosses the former main Leicester to Ashby-de-la-Zouch road (via Hugglescote) on the level, and to the north-east of this point originally stood a posthouse – the Ashby Road Hotel – from which a room was rented for station business.

From opening the station was known as Ashby Road but was changed to Bardon Hill when the Midland took over running the line in 1847.

The station was used for the first 16 years not so much by the few local inhabitants, but by travellers between Ashby and Leicester, who changed modes of transport here between road and rail. This transposition lasted (though reduced when Long Lane opened) until the line was extended to Ashby in March 1849, at which time Bardon Hill station was closed.

Closure proved to be only temporary, however, as the station reopened on 1 September 1849 when the line ran through to the more useful station at Campbell Street, Leicester rather than West Bridge. Passengers also had use of platforms constructed south of the crossing in that year.

Again in 1849, with the railway having reduced considerably the normal business of the hotel, the whole building was leased by the Midland Railway who were to use it for station offices, Station Master's house and waiting rooms. Eventually the Railway Company purchased it outright.

The platforms were lengthened in 1861 and generally enlarged in 1874, but waiting shelters were not provided until 1883, when almost identical,

A 1951 view looking towards Coalville showing the former Ashby Road hotel - used as the station offices at Bardon Hill. (Stations U.K.)

The platforms at Bardon Hill, 1951. (Stations U.K.)

enclosed, timber sheds with single sloping roofs were built each side of the line. The booking office was extended in 1903.

The two-storey hotel building was used, although in a rather dilapidated condition, until the station's early closure from 12 May 1952. There are now no signs of any part of the station.

COALVILLE TOWN

This was the last of the Leicester & Swannington stations and like most others on the line was by a level crossing. The road crossed was originally called Long Lane (now Hotel Street), then in the parish of Whitwick.

The first of three stations to appear on the same site was merely a stopping point north of the crossing, and originally called Long Lane, but was changed to Coalville (a name used for the area since about 1835) soon after the Midland took over effectively in 1847.

Concurrent with the station's opening the Railway Hotel was built at the crossing, and a room rented where passengers could book and wait for their train. An imminent arrival was con-

veniently announced by the ringing of a bell inside the hotel.

Similar to the situation at Ashby Road station, horse carriages from Ashby-de-la-Zouch met the trains here until Ashby had a station of its own. For a short time, from 1839 to 1840, the carriages also went as far as Burton to connect with London-bound trains, but from 1840 (until the line's southern extension in 1849) it was quicker for Coalville passengers to reach London by changing stations (West Bridge to Campbell Street) at Leicester.

With the doubling of the track by the Midland in 1848 a new station was built with the main building on the Down side. It consisted of two, pitched-roof buildings at right angles to the track, the one to the north two-storey, the other single-storey, joined by a short single-storey bay. The basic design was similar to the existing Moira building, the most notable feature being the heads of all openings in the four-centred style, with matching dripstone hoods.

There followed many alterations to the station which showed its increasing importance as the

Bookings were first carried out in the Railway Hotel, shown on the right in the Coronation year of 1910. The station signal box at Coalville gave clear views of road and rail.

A faded print showing the Coalville station in use between 1848 and 1900.

Typical Midland Railway architecture of the turn of the century apparent at Coalville Town in 1956. (H. C. Casserley)

A 1965 view from the Up platform at Coalville Town. (R. Gulliver)

town grew: there was a footbridge added in 1851, a waiting room in 1858 and a large waiting shed erected on the Up platform in 1865. The Station Master had a new house built in High Street during 1869, his accommodation at the station being converted into further waiting rooms and offices. Among other alterations were extensions to the platforms in 1875 which were then raised in 1882 and a metal footbridge provided the following year.

Even so, the Coalville public were not satisfied with their 'inadequate station' and from 1894 regularly petitioned for a new station 'complete with awnings'. They did have their way, although the station took nearly two years to build before completion in the summer of 1900.

The new single-storey building was typical of Midland design of the period; gable ends were raised above the roof line (stone-capped and topped with ball finials), there were stone string courses and terra-cotta mouldings that included a large 'MR' moulding let into the wall at the road end. The public were also granted their request of cantilevered awnings (glazed and with hipped ends) over both platforms – and over the main

entrance – although the latter did not last the lifetime of the station.

The main building seemed no larger than the one it replaced, however, although on the Up, Leicester platform, there were much improved waiting facilities. A dominant feature on this platform was a large, brick-based water tower. 'Town' was added to the station title from 2 June 1924, probably to distinguish it from Coalville East station which, by then, was also part of the LMS.

Despite being well used, the station closed with the line's passenger service in 1964, the buildings lasting until 1976. The only remains of the station are part of the Down-side platform containing a piece of station building wall, and the terra-cotta 'MR' which is preserved at Shackerstone station. The Railway Hotel was converted into offices in 1995 and, because of its historical interest, is now a Grade II listed building.

SWANNINGTON

The early Midland station buildings nearly always incorporated the Station Master's house which made even the country stations seem rather large.

Swannington in 1949 looking towards Leicester. (National Railway Museum)

The impressive platform shelter at Swannington, 1949 (R. E. Tustin)

A 1971 road side view showing the individual design of Swannington. (R. Gulliver)

Swannington is a typical example and had a grand appearance considering the small village it served. It had its own individual style, being cruciform in plan, with all sections two-storey, although not all of the pitched roofs were of the same height. The original windows all had stone quoins.

It was not opened with the northern section of the Burton line, but was delayed for six months until 1 September 1849 when the southern end of the line to Knighton Junction had been completed. It was situated west of the level crossing on the south side of the village and there were no goods facilities.

In 1860 a small waiting shelter was provided, and the platforms extended the following year. In 1871 a much larger, enclosed waiting room of brick and timber with diagonal boarding was then built on the Down platform, and a matching, but smaller room provided adjacent to the main building. The platforms were again lengthened in 1873.

Traffic was always light, however, and this was the first station on the Leicester-Burton line to close, which occurred from 18 June 1951. The empty station building lingered for several years but finally disappeared in the early 1970s.

ASHBY-DE-LA-ZOUCH

Here was the most elegant station frontage on the line and of the smaller stations probably the most elegant in the County. This was a result of Ashby aspiring to become an important spa town, and the railway anticipating an influx of fashionable people passing through the station on their way to the grand Ivanhoe Baths. The baths were opened in 1822 and located opposite to where the station approach road was built south of the town. They were in single-storey classical Greek style, a design that was matched by the stone station (still standing), and attributed to the same architect, Robert Chaplin.

The station's frontage is very long featuring the main entrance with pair of Doric columns flanked by sections linked to the entrance by bow-fronted bays. The frontage then extends eastward terminating with another similar bay. Beneath the building at this end is a basement which contained offices, and at one time, incorporated stables.

A large skylight resembling a Greek temple surmounted the grand entrance, although it became unsafe and was removed by about 1950. However, the station was not so elegant on the platform side where the canopy, added shortly after opening, comprised five semi-circular sections of corrugated iron.

The station was opened with the line on 1 March 1849 and changed very little over the years, although activity was increased in the booking office from 1874, when the branch to Derby was opened (Section 5). This line was served by a remote platform at the end of the branch, west of the station site.

In 1874-5 the main platforms were extended eastward, the sections over the road bridge being of timber, and both subsequently raised in 1903. A boarded crossing (surprisingly no footbridge here) gave access to the Down side where the large waiting room block, in typical 1870s Midland style, had a partially open front protected by an overhanging hipped roof that formed a small canopy.

On the station approach – a large cobbled area – was the tram terminus of the Burton and Ashby Light Railways (1906-27). This company was also owned by the Midland Railway, and offered an alternative route to Burton although somewhat more circuitous. Traces of the tram track remain on the approach. Now removed from the right-hand side of this area is the two storey station house.

Ashby (changed to Ashby-de-la-Zouch in Ashby-Nuneaton timetables in October 1923 and in Leicester-Burton timetables in January 1925) was always a busy station and even had a bookstall for many years, but it closed with the line's passenger service in 1964. Its elegant frontage is now a Grade II listed building tastefully renovated for use as a house and offices.

Ashby-de-la-Zouch as desirable offices in 1986. The door on the left side has replaced a window.

Houses now block this view showing the lower floor at Ashby-de-la-Zouch, 1970. (R. Gulliver)

The raised skylight can be seen and the less impressive corrugated-iron awning on the Ashby-de-la-Zouch Up platform.

Another view of Ashby-de-la-Zouch in 1956.
(H. C. Casserley)

MOIRA

The station still stands at the end of its own drive on the north side of the Ashby Road. The main structure that was opened with the line in 1849 comprises two bays in 'T' formation, both two-storey with pitched roofs on which the gables had typical Midland decorated bargeboarding. Accommodation for the Station Master was included.

The windows are the most attractive feature, with three, pitched-roof dormers, and the remainder mullioned of the four-centred style with stone drip mouldings. Heads of the doors were similarly styled. It was a building worthy of a small spa town as Moira had been since 1815.

There were plans approved for waiting rooms and alterations in 1862, 1866 and 1870, but it is not clear which parts of the building were added on which date. One addition was a single-storey section on the road side of the main building blending in well by using the same style windows and similar corbelled brick course. Another was a waiting room, probably that on the east side, although a minute referring to an additional waiting room also refers to an extra bedroom of which there is no evidence. There was an extra bedroom created however, some 40 years later when an additional dormer window was added on the platform side.

Platforms were lengthened in 1872 and raised in 1902. Also in 1902, a single-storey booking hall was added to the west bay, although not of matching style on this occasion. The porter's accommodation varied; in 1893 a disused signal box at the end of the platform was converted for their use, and in 1921 the appearance of the station was marred by the use of a goods van body which also doubled as a parcels office until station closure in 1964.

The main station buildings can still be seen but in derelict condition. They were sold by British Rail in 1991 and would require major repairs before they could be habitable again. Application for a preservation order has been raised but so far the building is not listed. The substantial pitched-roof shelter that stood on the Up platform has been removed.

Midland traffic returns in the appendix show that at one time there was a very high usage for this station considering its size of catchment area. Receipts were comparatively low, however, indicating that mostly short journeys were made –probably to Ashby and Burton.

The Down platform at Moira eight years before its 1964 closure. The signal box was redundant at this time. (H. C. Casserley)

Plain buildings flank the original at Moira, 1974. (Michael Mensing)

The road side of Moira in 1968.
An early additional bay is on the right, a later one on the left.
(R. Gulliver)

KIRBY MUXLOE

Surprisingly there was no station provided on the southern section of the through route to Burton when it was opened for passengers on 1 August 1849. Not until 1 June 1850 was a stopping place shown in the timetable, actually in Kirby Fields (near to where Towers Close now stands), but oddly called Braunston (without an 'e'), which was about two miles away. There was no evidence of a shelter or even a platform being provided. Similar to Leicester & Swannington practice, tickets were issued from a nearby ale house, the Blue Pots, which was originally a farmhouse. Adjacent to this and opened at approximately the same time was a private goods wharf owned by Joseph Ellis, an employee of whom, not only ran the wharf but was also hired by the Midland Railway to act as Station Master, signal man, porter and clerk! The wharf area, always known as Blue Pots, was sold to the Railway Company in 1885.

Meanwhile, a permanent station had been built about ¼ mile to the west, opening on 1 July 1859,

An early view of Kirby Muxloe taken from the signal box.

and the name changed to Kirby Muxloe. It was built on land belonging to a large house, Forest Ville (later The Towers), the owner of which insisted that a private path was provided from his house to the station where a small gate led onto the platform. The station was normally approached by a short drive from the main road west of the village.

The building provided was rather plain by Midland standards, consisting of a two-storey, L-shaped Station Master's house with single-storey offices attached to the west side. At the centre-front of the offices was a distinctive peaked gable. Oddly, the gables on all roofs had only shallow plain bargeboards which would normally, on Midland buildings at this time, be very decorated indeed. Each gable apex was topped with a spiked finial, and windows round-headed, characteristics which show shades of C.H. Driver's designs for the Leicester and Hitchin line two years earlier.

Alterations carried out were platform lengthening in 1873 and the provision of large brick waiting rooms on each platform in 1888. There were also large modifications to the station house in 1884, 1892 and 1919, and from World War II days a grounded carriage was used for storage at the east end of the Down platform.

At the end of the 19th century, passenger traffic increased rapidly here – especially from season ticket holders – with Kirby Muxloe growing to become an important residential area. Commuter traffic, mostly to Leicester, remained high until the end.

Prolific gardens were always a distinctive feature on the platforms – enhanced by neatly-cut hedges – but all were removed when the buildings were demolished about two years after the 1964 closure. This left only a farm crossing that was at the western end of the platforms to locate the station site.

Kirby Muxloe looking towards Coalville in 1959. (Les Hales)

Another view of the main building a year after closure. Stone sleepers from the Leicester & Swannington Railway can be discerned in the platform face. (R. Gulliver).

**MIDLAND COUNTIES
RAILWAY**

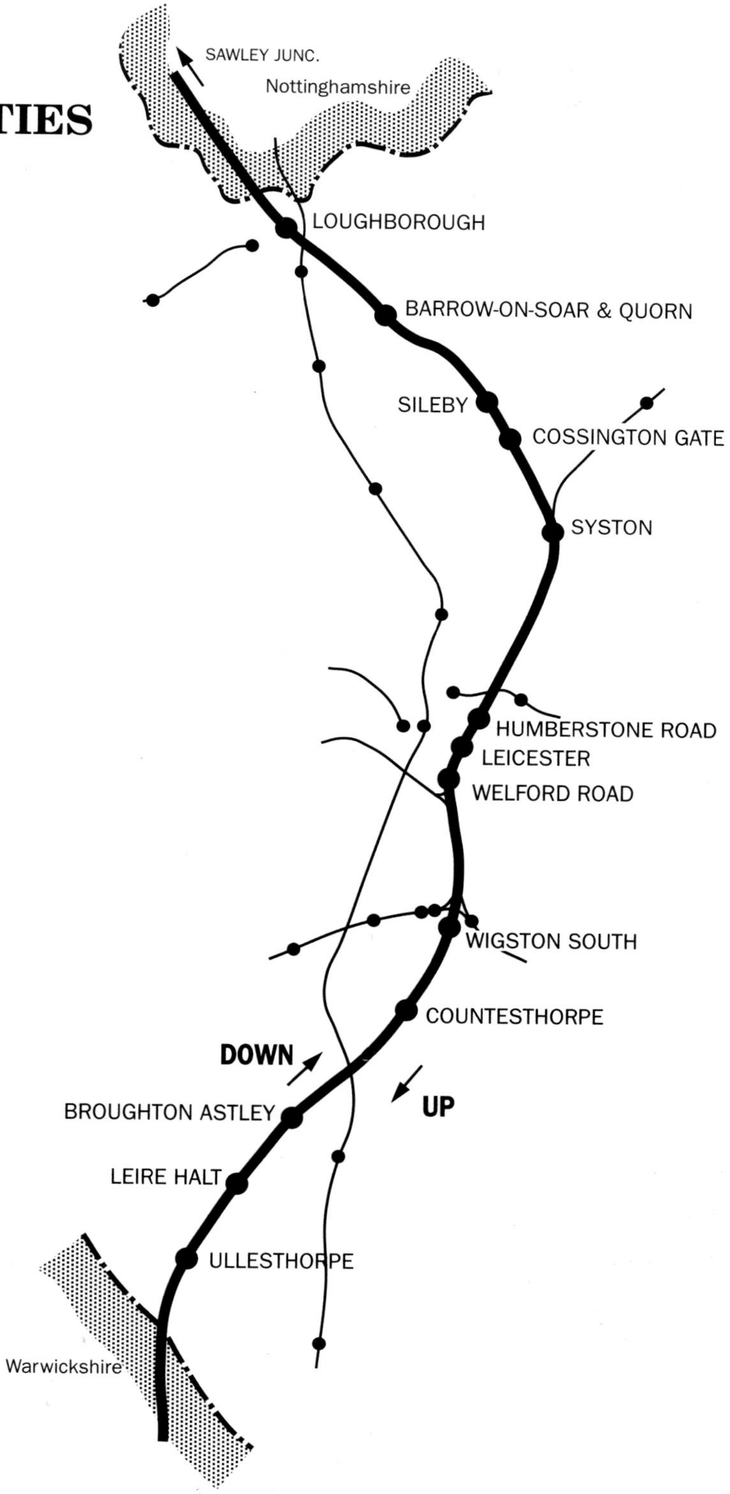

SAWLEY JUNC.

Nottinghamshire

LOUGHBOROUGH

BARROW-ON-SOAR & QUORN

SILEBY

COSSINGTON GATE

SYSTON

HUMBERSTONE ROAD
LEICESTER
WELFORD ROAD

WIGSTON SOUTH

COUNTESTHORPE

DOWN

UP

BROUGHTON ASTLEY

LEIRE HALT

ULLESTHORPE

Warwickshire

MIDLAND COUNTIES
RAILWAY

This line was opened in two sections through Leicestershire in successive months. The first was from Sawley Junction to Leicester on 5 May 1840, although a celebration special had run from Nottingham to Leicester the previous day. The initial train on the second section, to Rugby, was run for company personnel only on 18 June 1840 on the single line that was then available, with the services proper, including the London service, commencing on 30 June when the second track had been completed.

In the County, eight stations were opened with the line, although it was over two months after opening that all buildings were actually complete. Three of the stations — Barrow, Wigston and Broughton were of the same basic design, and from their costs of construction Sileby and Syston were probably very similar. They would all have been single-storey, fairly small (only slightly larger than the original crossing-keeper's houses at Cossington, Countesthorpe and Willey), with shallow hipped roofs, and square drip-stones over the openings.

Also common were the iron-latticed windows which, along with decorated bargeboarding used on MCR stations between Derby and Nottingham, were to become features appearing in many buildings of the Midland Railway (of which the MCR had become a constituent in 1844). The other three stations at Loughborough, Leicester and Ullesthorpe were individually designed.

The line is famed for the introduction of excursion trains, but these had actually run for many years on other railways (including the Leicester & Swanninington) before the claimed inaugural one from Nottingham to Leicester on 20 July 1840. More importantly, the world-famous Thomas Cook ran his first excursion on this line which departed from Leicester for Loughborough on 5 July 1841.

The line was built as double track with two goods lines added, mostly on the Up side, from Wigston northwards during 1873-4 (although Knighton Junction to Leicester was completed as late as 1892-3). This had little effect on the main station buildings, however, which were all on the Down side of the line, except for the small station at Cossington, which was eliminated altogether.

Cossington was in fact one of five minor stations provided since the line opened, and there was one station proposed but never built: In 1900, Leicester Corporation requested a station in Knighton Fields Road, Aylestone Park, where many new houses were being built and from where residents could quickly travel to Leicester. The Corporation even provided their own plan and estimate, but the Midland Railway found the proposal uneconomic.

From the Midland's traffic figures in the appendix, the high usage of the stations, particularly at Syston, is evident. Syston had more bookings than Melton Mowbray and sold substantially more season tickets for its size than anywhere in the County — strong evidence of a commuter area.

Only the section south of Wigston has closed altogether, where all traffic ceased and stations closed from 1 January 1962. North of Wigston, local services were discontinued from 4 March 1968 with only Leicester and Loughborough continuing to be served.

Some of the stations have been resurrected, however, with the starting of the 'Ivanhoe Line' — a project designed to reintroduce local trains with a service between Loughborough and Burton-on-Trent via Leicester. Station facilities (effectively halts with modern style shelters) have been provided at Barrow-on-Soar, Sileby and Syston, also an extra platform at Loughborough. Services started initially between Loughborough and

Leicester on 27 May 1994 with the trains on this section normally running on the slow lines:

LOUGHBOROUGH

The first of two station buildings on the site, that of the Midland Counties, still survives and can be seen south of the Nottingham Road bridge on the Down side. It is now preserved as a residential property after several years of neglect during industrial use.

Its squarish, two-storey design, although not particularly distinguished, resembles the first MCR station offices at Nottingham with square-headed windows and central door; but it differs in having a twin hipped roof, and originally had one single-storey bay on the east side. At Nottingham the roof was balustraded and flanked by two bays.

Improvements were frequent as its importance grew with the town, especially in 1858 when substantial modifications to offices and integral Station Master's house were carried out and new

waiting shed provided, the total cost amounting almost to that of the original station. The platforms were lengthened and raised in 1864.

The building was still inadequate for the town's needs, however, and a new station, the existing one, was built on the same side of the line, north of the road bridge. This opened on 13 May 1872 and the old building retained as the station house until about the time of the Second World War.

The new buildings, of unique design, comprise a single-storey, central bay flanked by lower, longer bays set forward towards the track both with dentils below the cornice. Each section has a hipped roof, round arched openings with stone surrounds on the road side, and in white brick with blue brick quoins. This splendid building is spoiled only by its industrial setting.

The station's other attractions are the original ridge and furrow awnings of iron and glass, supported on slender, fluted columns with decorated

An engraving made in 1840 of Loughborough's first station.

The original Midland Counties building at Loughborough taken in 1991 after renovation.

35

Plenty of ironwork evident at Loughborough in 1951 – facing south. (National Railway Museum)

Only parts of the screen on the Down platform remain at Loughborough in 1988.

spandrels, and a screen of similar materials on the platform side of the booking office. The glass has long since been removed from the screen, which once ran the full width of the central bay, and in recent years the hipped ends of the awnings, including spiked finials, have also disappeared. Once there was a glass canopy running the width of the central bay over the road-side entrance.

Perhaps because of the long platforms (those serving the new station joined those which served the old station under the road bridge), there were once two footbridges. One was built with the new station adjacent to the road bridge giving access to the road, and the other, the existing metal bridge, added very soon afterwards at the north end.

Originally known as just Loughborough, the suffix Town was added in 1923 for a short time, and then in the same year changed to Loughborough Midland. It was Loughborough again in 1970. It has also been known as Nottingham Road, but officially this only applied to the goods station between 1923 and 1950.

More modern events include the erection of a plaque to commemorate Cook's first excursion; a Grade II listing in 1981 (although the original station is not listed); tasteful restoration of the booking hall completed in 1984; and the raising of platforms in 1988. A W.H.Smith bookstall has also been removed for preservation at Loughborough Central and in conjunction with new local services, a short extra platform was

Loughborough's second station is externally little changed since building except for a much smaller glazed canopy.

completed in 1994 at the rear of the north end of the Up platform.

BARROW-ON-SOAR & QUORN

This was approached from a short drive north of the High Street and was the only station to retain its original Midland Counties character right through until the Beeching closures. It was single-storey with shallow, overhanging hipped roof which revealed shapely eave brackets. Doors and the iron-latticed windows had square drip-stones, and strengthening piers featured along the walls.

As well as containing booking office and waiting room, this small structure originally housed the Station Master, but in 1868 a separate, two-storey house was built to the north of the site, and the original domestic accommodation converted into waiting rooms. Between 1872 and 1874, at the time of track quadrupling, the station building

and platforms were enlarged and an enclosed waiting shelter erected on the Up platform. The building enlargement was at the north end, almost doubling the accommodation, and blending in well with similar roof and the same distinctive windows. A separate, matching lamp room was also erected at the north end. Further along the platform was the signal box, the standard type being replaced in 1919 by a much taller design to enable the signalman to clearly see the freight lines while passenger trains were in the station.

There was always a bridge carrying a public foot-path across the northern end of the platforms, the bridge being especially long when extended to span the goods yard sidings and new freight lines. It gave access to both platforms.

The station appeared in timetables as Barrow until May 1871 and Barrow-on-Soar until July

Several of the Midland Counties stations on the line were of this type seen at Barrow-on-Soar & Quorn in 1955.
(V.R. Webster)

A 1968 view at Barrow-on-Soar, looking south. (Andrew Muckley)

The new station, now called Barrow-upon-Soar, a year after its 1994 opening.

1899 when, with competition from the Great Central's new Quorn & Woodhouse station, it was renamed Barrow-on-Soar & Quorn. A lot of money was spent on raising the platforms in the early 1960s, rather late considering that closure came when local traffic ceased in 1968. The fine old station building was removed just a few weeks after closure and only the footbridge now remains. The main building area has been turned into a car park, and the sidings and site of the station house is now part of a housing development.

Because of insufficient space for platforms either side of the freight lines, this site was not chosen as a stop on the 'Ivanhoe Line'. Instead two platforms have been provided in the cutting ¼ mile further south. There is a new footbridge linking the platforms with access from Grove Lane but essential car parking facilities are lacking in this area.

SILEBY

The MCR did not intend to erect its own building here, but utilise two rooms in a house they had specially purchased. A month after the line opened, however, we know that the first payment was made to a builder for the erection of a station, so the decision to use existing premises must have fallen through. The type of building erected is uncertain, but the total payments made to the builder amounted to a figure almost the same as the cost of the smaller stations on the line like Barrow-on-Soar, and so was probably of similar design.

It was situated on the south side of King Street, west of the line and at the base of a steep embankment from which an inclined footpath gave access to the platforms. These platforms were widened and lengthened in 1858.

In 1864 a lengthy set of waiting rooms, supported on piles, was built on the embankment behind the Down platform. It was an early version of Midland wooden buildings with vertical panelling and large hipped roof which extended on three sides over the platform, but there is no indication of the usual valance. Four years later a replacement shelter that was erected on the other platform did have a deep valance at the front of a single sloping roof.

There was a wood and glass screen added to the main platform building in 1871 which could well have been to enclose an open-fronted central bay that became the booking hall. Also in that year the MCR building at street level was replaced by a rather plain Station Master's house of two storeys with pitched roof.

Access to the Up platform was by boarded crossing until 1912, when, after over 12 years of complaints, it was expensively replaced by steps from road level rising from a dim entrance beneath the adjacent bridge. Surprisingly, a simple footbridge was not used. At the same time, the area at the bottom of the embankment was cleared to allow station access from Brook Street, (regularly requested by residents since 1875), and the inclined path to the Down side platform moved to the south end of the platform building.

A further Station Master's house was built in 1913 on the opposite side of the road next to the Up line, allowing the one of 1871 to be used as a booking office and for handling the large amount of parcels business that originated here.

Station closure came with the ending of the local passenger service in 1968, but there were great efforts by the council to reopen, even while the platform buildings were being demolished early in 1969. They were, of course, unsuccessful.

The 1864 Down-side building at Sileby photographed in 1904.

Taken just before closure, the former Station Master's house which became the booking office in 1913. (H.E. Harrison)

*A view looking north showing
the long set of waiting rooms at Sileby, 1968.
(Andrew Muckley)*

*Looking in the same direction,
modern waiting shelters at the new
Sileby platforms in 1995.*

The Up platform entrance under the bridge was bricked up and debris from the platforms used to fill in the staircase. The road side booking office survived for a few years and at one time planning permission given for its use as a dental surgery. The only surviving building now is the 1913 Station Master's house.

Amazingly, the bricked-up staircase was opened up to access one of two new platforms provided for the reopening of the station in 1994. The other platform is reached from a new stairway on the Up side of the road-bridge — both platforms situated opposite those of the original station.

COSSINGTON GATE

The line originally crossed the Cossington to Seagrave road on the level, with a small, single-storey lodge erected for the gate-keeper to the north of the road, on the Up side of the line. This building became a station when, by public request, the Midland Railway allowed a Leicester train to stop on Saturday mornings with a return

working in the afternoon. The first service was on 1 December 1845.

Short, low platforms were provided despite its very limited use of normally two Saturday trains. Strangely this was reduced to just one Up train, with no return working, after about 10 years.

The building was removed to make way for the new goods lines and the crossing replaced by a road bridge. A proper station was thought uneconomic — the receipts quoted for the first five months of 1873 being only £3.0.7d — and so the station was closed from 29 September 1873.

SYSTON

Two station buildings have been erected on the site. The first was single-storey, and most probably similar to that at Barrow-on-Soar; but site plans show it to be slightly larger. It was situated east of the line, opposite to where the second station building now stands, with access from the Leicester Road goods yard entrance.

A road side view of
Syston's second station
in 1968.
(Andrew Muckley)

Soon after building it was realised that business for both freight and passengers was becoming far greater than anticipated. Many extra buildings were erected: warehouses, granary, stables etc. as well as a substantial enlargement of the station accommodation in 1842. The expansion continued after Syston became a junction station for the Syston and Peterborough Railway in 1846: platform shelters were enlarged in 1848, the main building was made two-storey with the addition of bedrooms for the Station Master in 1856, and the Up platform widened two years later.

Passenger accommodation was still insufficient and a much larger building was erected west of the line with access via Wanlip Road. It was completed in 1868 and has survived for use as industrial premises.

The style is one which became very popular on the Midland Railway, comprising three gabled pavilions, single-storey, and linked by pitched-roof bays with matching extension at the northern end. In its railway days the recesses formed by the bays on the platform side were roofed to form open porches. All gable ends still show decorated, open bargeboarding, and windows are of the rectangular, stone mullioned type — the overall style of building being very similar to the larger stations on the Settle and Carlisle line completed seven years later.

A year after the new buildings opened the Up platform shelter was replaced, and in 1872 a new Station Master's house (still existing) built by the new station. This replaced the residence at the original station which was then being removed because of track quadrupling. Further additions were a glazed, cantilevered canopy over the main entrance in 1873 and two years later a metal footbridge on brick piers situated midway along the platforms. Access was also provided to the narrow Up platform by steps from the road bridge at the south end.

An unusual addition of 1904, showing its continued popularity, was the provision of a second booking office on the Up platform. How long this remained in use is not known. On this platform was ample waiting accommodation with long waiting rooms and open-fronted shelters. There were no further alterations of note until the station

Passengers await a
south-bound train
in 1959 at Syston.
(Les Hales)

Humberstone Road booking office a month before closure. (Andrew Muckley)

closed with the local services in 1968 and the platforms removed.

On the resumption of local passenger traffic in 1994 only one platform was required. This is because the two slow lines to the south of Syston Junction had been reduced to one with bi-directional running. The new platform is, ironically, only a few yards from the original Midland Counties building, with the approach again from Leicester Road.

HUMBERSTONE ROAD

Unlike most large cities, Leicester did not possess any stations serving the populated parts of the centre, except at Humberstone Road, which was built to serve a large area of terraced housing and factories stretching eastward from the city.

It was not opened with the line, the plans being drawn up during construction of the freight-only lines, and a building for booking purposes provided adjacent to the bridge that spanned Humberstone Road. The building was at road level on the Up side of the line.

Opened on 2 July 1875, this structure was single-storey in a familiar, hipped-roof style with shapely eave brackets, the centre section of the rectangular building slightly recessed on the road side to give a 'twin pavilion' look. Enhancing the

Building decoration at Humberstone Road.

Humberstone Road platforms looking north, 1968. (Andrew Muckley)

design were decorative scrolls on the stone, square heads of the openings.

From this small building, passengers crossed a short yard before entering a dim tunnel beneath the tracks which gave access to two flights of steps each leading to very long platforms. The Up side was particularly long to enable use as a ticket platform, replacing one dedicated to ticket collection (opened 1845) that was situated north of the old Upper Fox Street bridge near Leicester station. Use as a ticket platform ceased, however, when Leicester became a 'closed' station, ie with ticket barriers, in 1918. Open timber waiting sheds were originally built on both platforms, but on the Down side a larger version with closed front was provided in 1900.

Although only small, the station survived until closure of local services in 1968. This may have been because it catered mainly for workers coming from north of the County to work in the vicinity of the station, rather than for the local population visiting Leicester, who were able to use the more convenient electric tram or bus services. (Regarding the tram service, when it opened in 1904, there was a marked effect on bookings at this station, quickly reducing them by about a quarter).

After closure, the platforms were reduced to rubble and used to fill in the stairways, but the booking office survived for use by small, private businesses for about 15 years. It then stood empty and neglected, despite being a Grade II listed building, until sold to Leicestershire County Council for just £1. This ensured its preservation as it was then moved brick by brick for re-erection at Shenton station on the preserved 'Battlefield Line' (Section 9) in 1993.

There was never a station house at Humberstone Road, instead, various dwellings were rented locally.

LEICESTER

At the end of Campbell Street, off London Road, stood large iron gates opening onto a vast forecourt. This was the entrance to the Midland Counties' station, originally just one building containing all facilities, which ran parallel with the long single platform. It was quite an elegant affair.

Designed by Leicester architect William Parsons (sometimes wrongly attributed to William Flint), it had a Classical frontage comprising a portico of six columns (the outer ones square and engaged) supporting a large pediment with central clock. When built it was two-storey of eleven bays flanked by small single-storey lodges. There were well-blended additions to both the higher section at the south end and to the lodges, a part of which accommodated the Station Master.

On the ground floor were parcels and booking offices, waiting rooms for three classes and refreshment rooms, while upstairs were many administrative offices, including the boardroom of the MCR until the formation of the Midland Railway, when the headquarters moved to Derby. Also on this floor was a balcony overlooking the line.

Classical frontage at Leicester Campbell Street.

An Edwardian scene outside Leicester's London Road station.

Over the platform a ridged cover, supported on iron columns, ran the full length of the building, and, with the exception of a central portion, was large enough to cover the loop line next to the platform. Being a single platform, catering for traffic in both directions, the loop was necessary to leave the two main lines clear for through traffic, a central scissor crossing allowing trains to enter and leave the station whilst another train was standing at the platform.

This arrangement did not last for long, however. Because of the rapidly expanding Midland system traffic increased greatly through Leicester, necessitating many alterations including two major enlargements. Firstly, in 1857 the station was given a more conventional layout with the addition of a second platform. This allowed the erection of an unusual clerestory-style, overall, glazed roof comprising longitudinal ridge and furrow sections over the platforms with transverse ridged sections forming the higher centre piece. Secondly, in 1868/9 a further platform face was added, form-

ing an island on which was built the normal array of passenger facilities.

Also at this time, a permanent booking office was built for the LNWR whose trains had run to the station from Nuneaton since 1864. Further improvements were the lengthening of platforms in 1870 and 1878, provision of a footbridge following a fatal accident in 1872 (accidents on the railway were so frequent that there was a station ambulance at least until 1911) and a transverse ridge and furrow canopy for the outside platform in 1878.

Despite the alterations, and its impressiveness from the outside, the station was still unsatisfactory according to various local bodies, the most important being the Corporation, who petitioned for an improved station 'worthy of the town'. They even tried to press the Midland into erecting a new station jointly with the Great Northern who were building their own branch to the town at this time, but the Midland found cause to refuse. By

*End elevation of the
carriage area at Leicester.*

1882 the station was described prior to a visit by the Prince of Wales as 'one of the dingiest buildings of its kind in the Kingdom'. Heavy decoration was needed for the royal occasion.

With this pressure, and perhaps because of the rival Great Central's new railway planned through Leicester, the Midland condescended by 1889 to completely rebuild the station. Their own architect, Charles Trubshaw, laid out the plan of the new structure, which was basically the one we see today.

Leicester Campbell Street, as the old station had been entered in timetables since 1867, was removed, and the new, more convenient building, Leicester London Road, erected. Although only half built at the time, it was opened on 12 June 1892 by the Lord Mayor who took a train all the way to Humberstone Road station in celebration! It took another three years to complete all aspects of the station.

When the old building was removed, all platforms were re-positioned so it is difficult now to orientate old and new. Approximately, the old building stood where platform 1 is at the moment. The wooden platform, which stood opposite platform 1, was erected for mail and light goods traffic only and had nothing to do with the former station. Remnants of the first station, the stone pillars of a gated side entrance, can be seen at the end of Station Street.

Trubshaw's design for the new station consisted of a long carriage area facing London Road, punctuated by many iron-gated archways of differing size. Some were lavishly decorated with various shades of typical late Victorian terra-cotta. Included in the decoration was the naming of the larger pair of arches to the right for 'Arrivals', through which is now the taxi stand, and another pair to the left for 'Departures', which now leads to the short-term waiting area and booking hall through further arcading. Completing the

*Plenty of bargains advertised
in the carriage area during
the 1930s at Leicester.
(National Railway Museum)*

45

frontage (now a Grade II listed building) is a balustrade topped with urns, and at the western end the familiar domed, octagonal clock tower.

Before recent modernisation the booking hall had a central octagonal booking office which, until LMS days, had been strictly for Midland use. The LNWR had their own booking and Station Master's office in the northern corner of the hall. An attraction outside these latter offices for many years until the 1960s were two encased models. One was of a Thames-Clyde Express dining carriage, illuminated by placing a penny in the slot,and the other was of the 'Rocket' whose wheels would turn for another penny.

From the hall, passengers pass the site of the ticket barrier, in use until the station became 'open' on 1 October 1984. At this point a large IRA bomb exploded in July 1939, causing much damage, especially to the show-cases (advertising Leicester's diverse trades) which were once a permanent feature on the adjacent, enclosed bridge that spans the lines. The bridge gives access to the two island platforms by wide, covered staircases.

For passengers arriving by train, there were, until recent modernisation, further flights of wide steps from the south ends of the platforms leading directly to the taxi stand in the carriage area —

The octagonal booking office at Leicester in 1985 just before its demolition.

The last days of ticket collection at Leicester, 1984. Notices announce the imminent change to an open station system.

Former exit to the car park at the south end of platforms 1 and 2 taken in 1985.

hence the term 'Arrivals' over the arches opposite this area. At the top of the steps were ticket-collecting booths, and at the side of them large baggage lifts. In latter years, however, these dingy exits fell out of general use and were only employed for excursion trains and specials.

At platform level, the 1892 buildings were all single-storey except for a second floor above the restaurants on each platform that provided sleeping accommodation for late-night staff. The Station Master was not housed at the station, the Midland Railway providing a residence about ¼ mile away in New Walk.

On platforms 2 and 3, buildings were all faced with colourful and decorated glazed bricks (as was the booking hall) and contained not only the usual

facilities, but until the inter-war years, provided less familiar services for passenger comfort such as foot-warmers, the hiring of cushions and rugs, and the selling of food hampers (empty hamper baskets were left in the carriages for return to Leicester). Beneath the buildings were cellars, reached by steps from the platform ends, and used as air raid shelters during the last War.

Also on the platforms, approximately half way along, were two signal boxes, Leicester East and Leicester West. Both had projecting bay windows over the two platforms they served, and at the side of each was a large brass bell that rang loudly the code of an impending train — useful for passengers as well as staff. The boxes ceased operation in 1970.

London Road station platforms, about 1910.

47

Leicester station frontage, 1983. The travel and parcels offices were in the building on the left.

Looking south in 1970 from Swain Street bridge, Leicester. (M.A. King)

A contrasting view from the same vantage point taken 27 years later.

The original glazed bricks can still be seen at the entrance to the booking hall at Leicester.

All four platforms were covered, the inner ones by a longitudinal, triple-bay, overall roof that was glazed and very similar to the scaled-down version that still covers the carriage area. In 1941 much of the glass in the overall roof was shattered when a German bomb exploded in adjacent Conduit Street and all the glass subsequently removed. It was replaced with corrugated sheeting, but only immediately above the two platforms. There was a deep screen at the northern end of this roof.

Cantilevered ridge and furrow glazed awnings with hipped ends covered the outer platforms and also both ends of platforms 2 and 3, as the overall roof did not extend the full length of all buildings.

As well as the main passenger bridge at the 'business' end of the station, there were two others. At the northern end was a footbridge reached by two covered stairways from the platforms and allowed access to separate points either side of Swain Street bridge. This useful amenity was removed when Leicester became a 'closed' station on 1 February 1918. The other bridge, still in use, links both platforms with the Postal sorting office via lifts, although it can be used for luggage and by less active passengers to gain access to the booking hall.

The suffix London Road was dropped from timetables commencing 4 May 1970, since when radical changes have taken place at the station. Firstly, in 1975 the overall roof was removed followed by the erection, the following year, of incon-gruous corrugated flat roofs which covered only half the width of platforms 2 and 3. Fortunately they were only temporary, for starting late in 1978 most of the buildings on platforms 3 and 4 were completely replaced by the present modern brick structures with integral deep awnings. This was repeated on platforms 1 and 2 soon after.

Although these new buildings were finished in 1982, there were still disused buildings at the southern end which took another ten years to demolish and for the platform modernisation to be concluded. During this time the booking hall was completely renovated. It now incorporates a travel centre, which had previously been in a separate office outside the station, and a new booking office situated on the northern wall. This re-vamped area was opened officially on 30 May 1986 by the Prince and Princess of Wales.

The last additions of note were a footbridge in 1989 to link the northern ends of the platform buildings with a new car park at the side of the station, and a year later a stairway for football supporters to access the carriage area directly from platform 2.

WELFORD ROAD

In 1872 the Leicester cattle market was moved from the centre of the town to a site between Aylestone Road and Welford Road. It was conveniently next to the railway, and a short branch for cattle trucks was built under Welford Road into the market. Mainly because of pressure from the Leicester Corporation, a station for farmers

The station at Welford Road was advertised in the foot notes of some Midland Railway timetables.

Welford Road platform in 1891 with the new bridge to accommodate track quadrupling under construction. (National Railway Museum)

attending the Wednesday and Saturday markets was also provided, and situated on the main line between Welford Road bridge and Knighton tunnel.

Because it was to be used by both the Midland and LNWR, agreement was reached for the former to own the station and arrange the building, whilst the latter paid for the construction plus an annual rental of £20. Both companies used the platform virtually until closure, the Midland from Burton, Birmingham, Rugby and Kettering, and the LNWR from Nuneaton. After about 1899, the Midland services were unadvertised. Although listed in some early timetables in the local press as Leicester Cattle Market and also Knighton Road, Welford Road was the official title.

It opened on 4 November 1874, but oddly, a platform was provided on the Down side only — maybe because building of the new freight lines on the opposite side had been projected by this time. As it happened, the additional lines were not installed until 1893, but it was not, even then, thought worthwhile building a second platform to serve the few market-day trains. Farmers had, therefore, to make their way to London Road station (via a tavern or two?) to catch their return train. This situation was very unusual where passengers could arrive at, but not depart from a station.

Exit from the station was by a rising path from the end of the platform to Welford Road. At the side of the path stood a small wooden hut, probably for ticket inspectors who were employed here as the station also served as a ticket collecting platform for Leicester station.

In 1847 such a platform had been provided between New Walk and London Road for Down traffic to Leicester, but gradually fell out of use on the building of Welford Road. Not all tickets were collected at these platforms, however, as all three Wigston stations, Kirby Muxloe, Great Glen and even Coalville were also used for this purpose for certain Down trains. (Similarly for Up trains to Leicester, Syston was sometimes used rather than Humberstone Road, and for expresses from

alighted here en route to the racecourse, situated until 1883 on Victoria Park.

The platform was removed in 1985, and the path that led to it is now the entrance to a nature trail.

WIGSTON SOUTH

When the line opened, Wigston was a small village centred where Wigston Magna is now, so villagers travelled well over a mile to the new station, then amongst fields on Blaby Road. The building was situated north of a level crossing where now stands the Wigston Health Centre. The building, on the Down side, was single-storey, almost identical to the hip-roofed original at

Wigston South in 1961 looking north towards Leicester. (Stations U.K.)

Sheffield, tickets were occasionally collected at Loughborough. Further out still, Market Harborough, Melton Mowbray (MR) and Hinckley have been used for collecting from long-distance specials.)

Due to shortage of staff at these places during the First War it was necessary for all tickets to be collected at Leicester which was made a 'closed' station from 1 February 1918. Welford Road was also taken out of use for the farmer's stopping trains five days later, although tickets were still collected here on a few occasions after this.

The platform was subsequently used occasionally by football specials for supporters visiting Filbert Street. It is believed, but not verified, that to avoid congestion at London Road, the platform was also used in its early days by racegoers who

Barrow-on-Soar, containing booking office and small accommodation for the Station Master.

By 1859, two cottages for other railway personnel were built further along the platform, and in 1861 a small shed on the Up platform was replaced by proper waiting rooms. A year later a second storey was added to the station, but curiously only to the two-thirds of the building nearer the road, the remaining single-storey section appearing then to have been an attachment on the side. With the enlargement, the overhanging, hip-roof style with distinctive eaves was retained and piers continued to upper floor.

For it to be distinguished from the new Wigston station on the Leicester and Hitchin line (Section 4) the name was changed in 1868 from Wigston to Wigston South. This is significant because by

A view at Wigston South showing typical Midland Counties window design behind some of the station staff. (Leicestershire Record Office)

The Up staggered platform at Wigston South, 1960. (R. Wellings)

about 1884, the area around the station had become well populated and had the unusual distinction of being named South Wigston after the station. The large rise in population is apparent from the figures in the appendix where the average annual bookings rose between the periods 1872-4 and 1888-90 from 8,254 to 38,800.

The most changes to the station came in 1890 when the platforms were staggered. Blaby Road was becoming busy, and to allow the crossing gates to be opened as soon as trains had pulled into the station from both directions, the Up platform was moved to the south side of the road. The signal box was moved in the opposite direction, south to north and at the same time a metal footbridge erected south of the crossing. A small timber shelter was also provided on the new platform and much larger brick and timber waiting rooms

built on the Leicester side. The station remained thus until 1962 when closure came to the least used of the three stations that Wigston then possessed. All traces of South Wigston's origin was then gradually replaced by various building developments on both sides of the road.

COUNTESTHORPE

The intention was to open a station with the new line, but just when tenders were received for the building, the idea was suspended. Presumably it was to reduce costs, but savings would have been minimal as a crossing-house with keeper had to be provided on the site anyway, and this was probably only slightly smaller than the minor station that was planned.

The house was soon required to act as a station, however, its earliest known use for passengers being in June 1842 when a timetable footnote in the Leicester Journal announced that one train in each direction would call at Countesthorpe Gate House on Saturdays only. By May 1845 trains had increased to two each way on Leicester market days, and a year later the suffix Gate House dropped. Its increased stature is then shown by the lengthening of its two very low, facing platforms, and by an official notice declaring that it was to be included in the Company timetable with daily trains from March 1846.

The crossing was situated just to the west of where the Railway Hotel now stands with the station on the north side of the road. The house was on the Up side, its style similar to the known sin-gle-storey station designs at Wigston, Barrow and Broughton Astley, with the exception that it had a shallow bowed projection central on the line side, whereas on the stations proper, the projection was squared.

Like Wigston, the platforms were staggered when a new Up platform was built on the opposite side of the road, but not to increase the flow of road traffic here, as the alteration was very much earlier in 1865. It was probably more convenient to build south of the road than raise substantially the low platform in front of the station building.

In 1867 a new house was ordered by the Board for the Station Master, but there is no record of its

The very low Up platform can be seen on this postcard view of Countesthorpe. The Railway Hotel is still in business.

A substantial shelter was provided on the Leicester platform at Countesthorpe. (Neil Cossons)

*Rudimentary facilities
for gentlemen.
(B.J. Smith)*

building. Three years later, however, plans were drawn for a well blended addition of a second storey, like Wigston, on just two-thirds of the house, to give extra accommodation for the Station Master. The work was carried out in 1871 when also the living room was converted to a waiting room. At the same time the Down platform was raised and a year later on this platform an elaborate brick waiting room was built with pitched roof and central cross-gabled bay, all gables having decorated open bargeboarding.

Completing the alterations around the turn of the century was an office extension at the rear of the main building, and the replacement of a small open shelter on the Up platform by a much larger one with closed front.

Remaining until the end (1962) in front of the main building, was the very low Midland Counties platform, on which was an unusually low station signal box. Housing developments have now completely covered the site.

BROUGHTON ASTLEY

The original station building was another in the familiar single-storey MCR design and similar in size to Barrow. It was built at road level on the west side of the bridge that carried the line over Dunton Road. Two flights of steps led passengers from the station to the platforms at the top of the embankment.

Most of the original station building is still standing, but the appearance has changed a great deal. The most significant change was when a second storey, so common on the line, was added to the whole of the original building, but in this conversion, the new hipped roof was without overhanging eaves. It is thought the addition was car-

ried out in 1859 when company minutes show the approval of a tender for station improvements costing a similar amount to other enlargements of this type. In 1862 the steps to the platforms were replaced by an inclined path. Two years later a trivial but most unusual order was given for urinals to be moved further from the platform edge!

Station business moved in 1871 from street level to the Down platform, where a large new building was erected containing offices, booking hall, waiting room etc. It was a standard Midland design in wood supported at the rear on brick piers. It had a large hipped roof, overhanging the platform and sides and with a deep decorated valance. Similar buildings were at East Langton (1876) and on the Melton-Nottingham line (1880). As part of the alterations the platforms were rebuilt and lengthened, the Up one extending well over the bridge onto the opposite side of the road.

Unfortunately, the new station's wooden construction was its downfall, for in June 1932 the building was set alight, presumed to be by sparks from an engine, and was totally destroyed. Booking reverted to the building at street level which had been converted by then (probably after erection of the 1871 platform building) into three separate dwellings.

It was not until 1936 that any permanent structures replaced those destroyed. They were simple wooden waiting rooms, which appear to be of LNWR origin, and were transferred from a closed station elsewhere. The platforms were raised at the same time.

The booking office remained in the original MCR station building until closure in 1962, and since then the whole building has been converted into

The original booking office and Station Master's house was single storey at Broughton Astley. This view, taken early this century, shows the building with additional storey.

A postcard view of Broughton Astley. The main building seen on the Down platform was destroyed by fire in 1932.

A DMU bound for Leicester pulling into Broughton Astley, about 1962. (Neil Cossons)

The Up platform at Broughton Astley. (Neil Cossons)

one large house, its new openings and stucco finish completely hiding the original station design. Except for parts of the narrow platforms, all other traces of the station have disappeared.

In the early years, official naming of the station varied. Opening as Broughton, it became Broughton Astley in 1845, reverted to the original name in 1870 and nine years later was Broughton Astley again.

An unusual claim to fame is that the station was haunted. The ghost of a platelayer, who had been killed nearby, apparently continued to turn up at the station for his wages for many years.

LEIRE HALT

Although the railway ran close to the west side of Leire village, there was no station planned with the line as the area was so thinly populated. A first request for a station was made by the inhabitants of Frolesworth, Ashby Magna and Leire in 1897, but this, and many subsequent ones were declined. Right up to LMS days a station was not considered worthwhile, despite the village expanding. With two years of pressure from the

local council, however, and the council's willingness to pay approximately £100 to the cost, the railway company condescended to provide a halt.

At that time it was an unusual decision, for many country bus services were starting and the trend was for stations to close rather than open. However, on 2 March 1925 villagers welcomed their first train with flags waving and the band playing, and celebrated in the evening with bonfire, fireworks and grand dance.

The halt was reached by a footpath from the centre of the village, and consisted of two short concrete platforms. On the Down side was a small closed shelter of wood with single sloping roof and at the south end of the same platform was an asbestos lamp hut

Although called a halt, it was in fact manned for the issue and collection of tickets, and at one time for the handling of small goods, which included live chickens that left here in their thousands. One porter looked after everything including tending the oil lamps which were in use till the end.

Leire Halt in 1952 looking north. (National Railway Museum)

Accommodation (and lighting) was basic till the end at Leire Halt. The notice by the door delivers a religious message. (Neil Cossons)

Closure in 1962 was particularly disappointing because, despite its size, the halt was used more than most of the stations on this section of line south of Wigston. The platforms remained for about 20 years until removal and the area grassed over.

ULLESTHORPE

The first of two buildings provided here was very large for the size of village it served. Possibly the important town of Lutterworth, only 3¼ miles distant, had some bearing on its dimensions, but more likely it was the Chairman of the MCR, Thomas Dicey, living at nearby Claybrook House, that had most effect. The building was erected at the top of an embankment, south-east of the bridge carrying the main road to Lutterworth and, although single-storey, was twice the size (and cost) of the line's smaller stations, and approximately equal in cost to Loughborough.

An early engraving shows it to have had an individual design, comprising two long bays side by side, each with pitched roof and raised stone gables supporting decorated bargeboarding. Like most MCR buildings, there were square dripstones over the openings. The Up platform was reached by two flights of steps descending the embankment, each flight having a right-angle turn half way.

Although large, this building proved to be inconveniently situated, so for this reason at least, it was decided in 1870 to purchase land for a revised station layout. New staggered platforms were provided with just a board crossing between ends, and a new station building erected on the Down platform, then reached through the goods yard entrance. Completed in 1872, it was a plain building, long and single-storey with round-headed openings and pitched roof. On the other platform,

An engraving of the original station building at Ullesthorpe.

57

The Down platform at Ullesthorpe in 1961 including Station Master's house with lozenge-patterned windows.
(B.J. Smith)

Ullesthorpe's platform shelter was similar to Broughton Astley but of vertical boarding.
(Neil Cossons)

an elaborate timber shelter was provided with open front and single sloping roof.

Somewhat mysterious is the two-storey Station Master's house situated at the south end of the Down platform, for it is not mentioned, as far as is known, in company minutes, and so its building date is unknown. From its appearance, it pre-dates the new station building, but is later than 1852 as it is not shown on a plan of that date.

Residents of Lutterworth were frequent users of the station, and for well over 60 years a horse bus from that town always met certain trains. In fact, although the original station name was Ullesthorpe, it was suffixed in 1879 'for Lutterworth' (changed to 'and Lutterworth' in 1897) but in 1930 reverted to just Ullesthorpe.

The last alteration of note was in 1935 when both very low platforms were raised. Closure came with the line and all was removed, except for the station house, which now lies in the midst of a housing estate covering the station site.

SYSTON & PETERBOROUGH RAILWAY (MR)

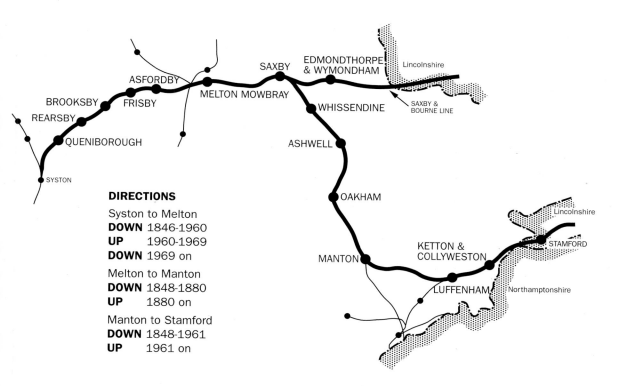

DIRECTIONS

Syston to Melton
DOWN 1846-1960
UP   1960-1969
DOWN 1969 on

Melton to Manton
DOWN 1848-1880
UP   1880 on

Manton to Stamford
DOWN 1848-1961
UP   1961 on

SYSTON & PETERBOROUGH RAILWAY (MR)

The Leicestershire section of the line was opened in two parts; from Syston to Melton for all traffic on 1 September 1846 and, because of problems at the infamous Saxby curve, the second part to Stamford not opened until 20 March 1848 for goods and 1 May 1848 for passengers.

The time of building was fortunate, because during this period, investment in new railways was particularly high, just before the 'mania' bubble burst, and so money was not too restricted on station buildings. With this, and the grand approach of the Midland's Chairman, George Hudson, the resulting variety and standard of architecture on this line has been particularly celebrated.

It could all have been so different with any further delays because during planning of the second section money was becoming scarce, shown by an instruction to the Company Engineer in April 1847 to decrease the number of windows in new and existing buildings and thereby reduce the payment of window tax. Overall station designs were not affected, however.

Responsibility for the architecture is not definite. Of the stations opened with the line, those on the first section to Melton were certainly by Leicester architect William Parsons, and we know that Francis Thompson (famous for his station designs in other parts of the country) was paid £800 in July 1847, almost certainly for station design elsewhere on the line. The Italianate flavour in the buildings at Oakham, Manton and Luffenham were in one of his favoured styles and most probably his work.

Of the remaining four, those at Saxby (first station), Whissendine and Ashwell had common features in their half-timbering and, although classified by the Construction Committee as third class stations, were far from third class in design. The other, at Ketton, had a very individual style in stone. It is probable, as part of his large fee, that these four designs were by Thompson also, but there is a possibility that the line's company architect, Sancton Wood, may have had some bearing on their style as he had designed many station buildings on other lines himself.

An interesting feature at the larger stations — Melton, Oakham, Manton and Luffenham (also Stamford, just outside the County) — was the use of galvanised corrugated iron for covering the platforms. It sounds today like a cheap and unsightly material, but in the late 1840s was virtually a new innovation and its use thought a worthwhile experiment despite it then being very expensive.

The route chosen for the line was moderately level, following river valleys most of the way, and therefore, with the exception of Manton, all original stations were adjoining level crossings. All main buildings had a two-storey section to include accommodation for the Station Master.

The line remains open, with the stations at Melton Mowbray and Oakham still used on the Railway network. Oddly, of the others, it was those in rural Rutland that remained open longest, until closure of stopping services from 6 June 1966, whilst those in Leicestershire closed between 1951 and 1961. Fortunately many of the elegant buildings on the line have survived.

Included in this section for convenience is Edmondthorpe & Wymondham, the only station in the County on the Saxby & Bourne line which branched from the Syston & Peterborough east of Saxby:

QUENIBOROUGH

This was not one of the line's original stations, but was built during the Second World War to serve the Rearsby Royal Ordnance Depot only and as

Peak class diesel D23 standing next to Queniborough island platform on which some of the spartan brick shelters can be seen in 1961. (J.C. Kirby)

such did not provide an advertised service. It was situated south of the Queniborough to Ratcliffe road (Broom Lane) though not accessible from it, in an area now known as East Goscote. It comprised a very long island platform set away east of the main running lines.

From the main lines access to the west platform face was possible from either direction, but the opposite face and the many goods sidings here could only be reached directly from the south. Both sides of the platform had run-round loops.

Waiting facilities were large but austere, with eight utility brick shelters equally spaced along the centre of the platform, each approximately 30ft x 6ft with flat concrete roofs suitable for doubling as air-raid shelters. They would only be used normally, however, when the evening train (on occasions two) was not ready and waiting for staff leaving the factory. The regular return service was from Leicester only, but for a short time a service ran through from Hinckley.

The station was first used on the 10 November 1941, but exactly when it closed is unknown — certainly near to the end of the War. Freight traffic was handled until the Depot closed around 1955 and the sidings then used for storage of coaching stock until the late 1960s. The site of the station now forms part of a landscaped area next to a new road, The Warren, which lies west of a housing estate that has replaced the Ordnance Depot.

REARSBY

The main station building, its design described as 'Victoriabethan', still exists for residential use. It was built west of the road to Thrussington on the south side of the line and originally comprised a two-storey Station Master's house and a single-storey booking hall joined by a low bay. The bay was subsequently raised in 1914 to form an additional bedroom which had dormer windows front and rear, matching a similar pair at the eastern end of the house. Plans for the enlargement could well have been those used at the almost identical

Rearsby from the north-west in 1948 only three years before closure. (Stations U.K.)

Elegant Rearsby, about 1959.

Asfordby station where a bedroom was added over 50 years earlier.

All openings are square-headed and all roofs steeply pitched. There are cross-gables at the front and rear of both buildings — originally with typical, decorated bargeboarding. In contrast the end gables are stone-capped as are the dormer windows. Important features of this elegant building were the tall, angled chimneys and lozenge-patterned windows, both sadly now removed.

Platforms were wooden until 1864 when they were replaced with 'ballast and asphalt', and the only other alteration of note was a low hipped-roof bay added to the western end.

The station was never well used and in the end an average of only three passengers per day were using the services. With Asfordby, it was first to close on the line — from 2 April 1951. There was no goods yard here.

BROOKSBY

There were so few houses at Brooksby that the station, sited east of the road to Hoby, was probably built mainly to serve Rotherby and Hoby, as well as the important Brooksby Hall. Serving this latter residence may account for such a large station, the cost of which was more than Rearsby and Asfordby together.

The station offices were in a long, single-storey block with the station house attached at the eastern end. The offices had a distinctive roof, hipped and deeply overhanging, the eaves decorated with wooden brackets that were large and elaborate. Peaked hoods in the roof also featured above the

An Edwardian view of Brooksby looking towards Melton Mowbray.

Another postcard view of Brooksby which shows the crossing-keeper's house on the left.

doorways at front and rear. Openings were mostly round-headed and dressed in stone, the windows narrow and generally in groups of three. Very tall chimneys topped the building matching those on the solid-looking large house, which also had a hipped roof, but its window heads were square. Both buildings had large stone quoins.

It was soon realised that the house was too large for the Station Master, for in 1847 there was an instruction to divide the house to accommodate a porter, and only two years later tenders requested for enlarging the porter's section. Another instruction was given in 1851 for the house to be divided yet again to make a separate tenement for a platelayer. Eventually the Station Master did have the house to himself after conversion of part of the station offices at the western end to house a railway employee. At the same end of the platform was a separate goods office and store. Except for accommodation modifications, the only other alteration recorded was the raising of platforms in 1890.

In contrast to the main building, the platform shelter opposite was a simple timber structure with single sloping roof.

Closure came from 3 July 1961, since when the house has sadly been demolished, but the station offices survive, externally intact and now used as farm buildings which are Grade II listed. A plain crossing-keeper's lodge of 1847 on the opposite platform survived until the mid 1980s.

FRISBY

Frisby village is adjacent to the line, but originally a station was not planned. Only six weeks after

The staggered platforms at Frisby in 1958 looking east. (Les Hales)

Frisby station house and booking office in 1983 a few months before demolition.

the line opened though, local inhabitants requested that trains for the Leicester and Melton markets be allowed to stop and an order was made for this to apply from 1 January 1847. At the same time, instructions were given for wooden platforms to be provided and a gatekeeper's house to be built 'sufficient for the market trains'. Building was complete by 28 May 1847 when architect William Parsons approved payment for its erection and also for provision of a platform waiting shed 'covered with patent corrugated iron'.

The two-storey, main building, situated east of the crossing on the north side of the village, was plain, with square-headed windows and hipped roof without eaves. It appears to be an adaption of a crossing-house design used at many locations on the line beyond Melton.

Not until 1 April 1849 did the station appear in the public timetable with a full service, although later that year it was reported 'trade was very low and station and gate could be put under control of platelayer and wife, the latter to attend to gates'. It is unrecorded if this was ever carried out.

Facilities were always very basic, booking being carried out in the front room of the house from where passengers walked to either of the remote, staggered platforms. On the platforms (the wooden ones replaced at some stage) were small open-fronted waiting shelters of timber, the one on the south side having an integral waiting room. By the crossing, on the opposite platform, was an enclosed ground-lever frame, replaced in 1941 by an LMS-style signal box.

Despite the meagre facilities, the station lasted until 3 July 1961. The platforms were soon removed, but the house remained occupied until demolished around 1984. There was never a goods yard at this station only a cattle dock for a short time after opening.

ASFORDBY

Situated west of the road running south of the village, this station was identical to Rearsby, with the exceptions that in plan it was a mirror image, and also the booking hall was larger, it extending on the road side. Even the addition of a bedroom for the Station Master above the central bay was the same, but here it was built much earlier, in 1862.

The platforms were staggered, but for reasons unknown were both on the same side of the level crossing. Uncomfortably for passengers, there is no evidence of there being a connecting board crossing. At the western end of the building was a separate, single-storey goods office and store similar to that at Brooksby.

On opening, the station was known as Kirby after the nearby hamlet of Kirby Bellars, but after reports of confusion with Kirkby, was renamed after the much larger but more distant Asfordby in December 1857.

In 1886 the Down platform in front of the main building was raised. This platform was unusually short at only 170ft — although sufficient for the small population it served. With traffic down to an average of only ten passengers per day, it closed

A 4F freight engine heading a Leicester-bound holiday special past Asfordby in 1959. (M.A. Cooke)

from 2 April 1951, demolition of buildings following some 16 years later leaving no trace of the station site.

MELTON MOWBRAY

When the line reached Melton the station buildings were incomplete and so a temporary stopping place was used (probably nothing more than a booking shed and crude platforms) which was sited close to the point where the line crosses Leicester Road.

The station proper was built west of a level crossing in Burton End. Its exact opening date is not known but J.Brownlow states in his book 'Melton Mowbray, Queen of the Shires' that it was ready in February 1847. An indicator to the station being completed that month is a report in the Stamford Mercury saying that on the 9th an engine was involved in an accident by mistakenly going to the old station instead of the new. The same month saw the start of a horse coach service to convey passengers between Melton and Stamford, the service lasting until the section of line linking the two towns was completed in 1848.

Difficult to understand is why the buildings provided at the new station were so plain, especially considering that Melton was in the heart of the lucrative hunting country and visited by gentry

Melton Mowbray looking west in 1969.
(John Bailey)

A 1984 road side photograph of Melton Mowbray showing the portico which was an addition to the original buildings.

Platform detail at Melton Mowbray, 1984.

from throughout the world. It was even inferior to other stations on the line, most serving much smaller communities.

The main buildings, mostly still existing, contained a two-storey, L-shaped section, flanked by single-storey bays, the one to the west long, and still containing the main entrance to the ticket office. The two-storey building, with hipped roof and plain square-headed windows, originally accommodated the Station Master until 1870. In that year, following many station alterations, he was temporarily housed in a porter's lodge until his own (Sycamore House) was specially built north of the adjacent goods yard.

A feature of the station was an overall roof of corrugated iron, but it lasted only until 1876 when, on 13 April that year, it came crashing down onto tracks and platform under an exceptional weight of snow. Although it happened in mid-afternoon no-one was injured, and trains were stopped in time to prevent a major disaster.

There soon followed, between 1879-81, the only large investments for the station — shown in company minutes merely for 'enlargements' — but these probably included the three-arched portico which was added to the front of the main entrance, and also the ridged glass canopies with their new rear supporting walls on each platform. The canopies are similar to those at the Midland's

Loughborough station (before the hipped ends were removed there), but are much less deep, covering narrower platforms.

Both additions improved the station considerably, and may well have been prompted by the new Nottingham to London main line which ran through the station from 1880 to 1966, and possibly by the building of the rival GN/LNW Joint station at Melton in 1879. The latter would not have created too much of a threat, though, as the only competing traffic was to Nottingham and Leicester, both much better served by the Midland.

In 1897 the present footbridge was added and at the turn of the century the busy level crossing replaced by a road bridge that also spans the adjacent river Eye. This was completed after 20 years of bitter campaigning by road users, the matter even being raised in Parliament. The crossing-keeper's house, single-storey and at the east end of the main platform, lasted until about 1960.

In 1938 just the platform on the north side was raised and lengthened, but it appears both platforms were still too short — a problem that lasted right up to the end of the direct London service — as many expresses wasted time having to pull up at the station twice.

In recent years the bookstall has been removed and the length of the glass canopies has been halved to reduce maintenance costs. The remote Station Master's house has also been demolished.

A stylish modernisation of the booking hall was carried out in 1986, but the removal of the single-storey buildings soon after at the eastern end, has tended to make the general appearance of the station plainer than ever.

The station nomenclature has changed on several occasions. Opening as Melton, it became Melton Mowbray in 1876, and Melton Mowbray (Midland) on becoming part of the LMS in 1923. It was Melton Mowbray (Town) in 1958, and finally, just Melton Mowbray in 1965.

SAXBY

Two stations have been built here, the second being necessary as the first was situated on a

A Bradford to St. Pancras express passing through the junction station at Saxby in 1955. The original station can be seen above the building on the island platform. (W.F. Deebank)

Saxby station from the south, 1955. (W.F. Deebank)

sharp curve (known as Lord Harborough's Curve) which was later realigned. The opening of the first station was not with the opening of the line — the station name appearing in timetables, but no service actually shown until 1 February 1849 — though why the delay, company minutes do not reveal.

The first station, approached by a drive from the Saxby to Melton road, has survived for residential use and is a large, two-storey building with pitched roof having cross-gables at the eastern end. It has half-timbered decoration, but some of the original has been lost with recent rendering. Although displaying none now, there were probably decorated bargeboards similar to the next two half-timbered stations on the line at Whissendine and Ashwell. The only alterations of note were in 1872 when a ladies waiting room and kitchen were added.

The second station, on the relieved curve, was built west of the new road bridge that was required between Saxby and Stapleford. It opened on 28 August 1892, although there had been goods traffic along the new track for some months before this. The original station building continued to house the Station Master, and its offices used for the goods business.

The main building at the new site stood on the north side of the line and was a standard Midland structure, single-storey, and comprising twin pavilions joined by a recessed bay. The platform side of the bay was in timber and glass and its full roof formed a porch supported by two wooden pillars. Roofs were pitched.

The new station area was very large — it was designed as a junction station in anticipation of the adjacent Saxby to Bourne branch opening the following year and also the track was quadruple at this point. It boasted three separate platforms, all reached by steps from the road overbridge, the central island platform having a large timber waiting room complete with flat roof. This roof overhung on all four sides, and with deep awnings was not unlike many LNWR structures. Being on an embankment, the platform on the south side was wooden, supported on piles, and complete with small timber shelter.

To the delight of the local population, an event that occurred for many Januarys in the 1900s was the arrival of the Royal Train from Chatsworth. The train was split here to allow King Edward VII to proceed to London and Queen Alexandra to Sandringham. There was always a good crowd, including local dignitaries, to view the Royal couple, the whole episode lasting about ten minutes.

Business was reduced when the Bourne Branch closed for passengers from 2 March 1959 and remaining services withdrawn completely from 6

February 1961. Most of the station was quickly removed but not the main brick building. Remarkably, this has survived unused, although is now reduced to a ruinous shell.

EDMONDTHORPE & WYMONDHAM

This stood on the Saxby & Bourne line which branched from the Syston & Peterborough Railway just east of Saxby. The branch opened for goods on 5 June 1893 and passengers on 1 May 1894. It was single track, although there was a loop at the station and, therefore, two platforms.

The station's delightful title was contrived from adjacent Wymondham, and, probably to distinguish it from the Norfolk station with the same name, included the more distant hamlet of Edmondthorpe. It was built nearly two years later than the second Saxby station, but the design of the single-storey main building was practically identical. The platforms were reached by similar timber steps from the adjacent road overbridge, but here, half-way along the platform, was a low signal box just east of the main building.

On the opposite platform was a small pitched-roof shelter of brick, glazed with many small panes — an unusual design for the Midland.

Closure came on withdrawal of the line's passenger services from 2 March 1959 when through goods on the line were also discontinued. Access was retained through the station to ironstone quarries until September 1967. Just the basic structure of the main building can still be seen situated east of the road between Wymondham and Garthorpe, and has been converted for use as a smart residence.

Edmondthorpe & Wymondham on the south side of the branch line to Bourne in 1958.
(Les Hales)

Lamp detail at Edmondthorpe & Wymondham.
(Neil Cossons)

An unusual style of platform shelter at Edmondthorpe & Wymondham
(R. Gulliver)

A picture taken at Whissendine in the 1950s when boys wore short trousers– and sometimes a watch chain. The partitioned platform shelter can be seen. (Stations U.K.)

Once a fine building, but soon became derelict after closure. Whissendine looking towards Melton in the early 1960s. (Stations U.K.)

WHISSENDINE

On opening this was known as Wymondham despite it being between two nearer places, Whissendine and Edmondthorpe — maybe at that time Wymondham was the more important village. No doubt, to avoid confusion with the similarly-named and larger Great Eastern station, it was changed after only four months to Whisendine (becoming Whissendine in 1878).

Considering the small populations it served the station was impressive, the dominant aspect of the large, two-storey building being its half-timbered decoration, but there were also many small details featured. These included the use of local Collyweston 'slates', finials on the gables of the pitched roofs (with chimneys of white brick), and diaper pattern-work of blue brick in the lower parts of some walls. There were also short brack-

eted shades over the square-headed windows and, of course, there was shapely bargeboarding.

The building was T-shaped in plan with attached, open-fronted waiting shelter parallel to the platform. Large pitch-roofed porches covered the entrances to the Station Master's quarters and the booking hall, the latter, open and enhanced by carved wooden brackets, the former comprising two small rooms which appear to be part of the house enlargements of 1874. On the opposite platform a third of the large, open-fronted waiting shelter was partitioned off in 1870 to form a small goods store.

The station sustained traffic until 3 October 1955, but from then Whissendine villagers could use Ashwell which was almost as convenient. The fine station building stood, sadly neglected, and

70

Taken early this century, Ashwell viewed from the south.

Ashwell in 1963 looking towards Oakham. A low platform is evident by the provision of steps – moved to the carriage door by request. (Stations U.K.)

latterly in quite ruinous condition, until demolished in 1984.

ASHWELL

This was located north of the road running due west of the village. It was another half-timbered building, but was different in arrangement to the previous two, comprising a two-storey section with single-storey bay at right-angles on either side. Connected to the track side bay were the main waiting rooms, with open recess showing timber roof supports at the front.

This part was similar to Whissendine, as were the window shades, patterned brickwork, and decorated booking-hall porch, although this was removed in later years. All roofs were pitched and covered with fish-scale tiles, including the substantial platform shelter which matched the platform side of the main waiting room with its open recessed front.

The only alterations of note were the addition of a waiting room in 1871 and creation of a bedroom the following year. This grand station closed with the line's stopping services in 1966 and buildings razed in the late 1970s. The site remains unused.

OAKHAM

This station is conveniently sited near the centre of the town, but near to a very inconvenient level crossing. A new road now runs in front of the main building which once overlooked a large forecourt that seemed more fitting for this elegant station.

The two-storey main building has a central bay flanked by two narrow pavilions, both set forward, their over-hanging pitched roofs at right angles to the bay. Large, shaped eave brackets feature, and with the upper windows in the pavilions narrow and round-headed there is an Italianate quality. Between the protruding pavilions is a portico of four square columns, and either side of the main structure are ancillary single-storey buildings with plain pitched roofs. White brick headings of all openings contrast with the buildings' red brick.

On the platform side, narrow iron columns support an awning of curved corrugated iron suitably hidden by a plain valance which has been reduced in depth. Beneath the canopy for many years was a bookstall, which was moved in the 1940s when a counter, facing onto the platform, was opened in an adjoining shop, although no longer in use. Accommodation on the opposite platform, probably that planned in 1869, started as a very long, open shelter of brick, at the rear of which can still be seen a central door giving access to Barleythorpe Road. In 1903 separate timber-fronted waiting rooms were made at each end of the shelter. Much later, the room at the southern end was removed, and the other end rebuilt.

Other late modifications include raising of the platforms (unusually arranged in a half-stagger), the Leicester one in 1913 and the other in 1938, when also both were lengthened. In the 1960s, the sturdy wooden footbridge that had linked the platforms at the northern end since around 1900 was replaced by one of metal, though this is rather plain compared with the ornate metal one of 1901 which still serves the level crossing just south of the station. The main station building is now listed Grade II as is the Midland-style signal box by the crossing.

Italianate facade at Oakham, 1961. (Neil Cossons)

The Peterborough platform at Oakham in 1989.

Half-staggered platforms and inconvenient columns still supporting a corrugated iron canopy at Oakham. (Lens of Sutton)

MANTON

The Midland did not intend the line to pass near Manton originally, but Uppingham residents, keen to have reasonable access to a railway, persuaded the company to re-route and build a station at Manton conveniently 3$^{1}/_{2}$ miles from Uppingham. From opening, therefore, the station was listed as Manton for Uppingham, the suffix lasting until 1950 in British Railways' timetables and in Bradshaws for a further ten years.

Two station buildings have been erected (both still existing for industrial use) and reached by a very long drive from the Manton to Wing road. The first is a fine two-storey building of rendered brick, cruciform in plan, each wing with projecting pitched roof and cornice decorated with curved brackets. Windows are square-headed, though on the road side, the first floor windows and doors are rounded. There are also single-storey bays attached to the side wings, although they appear to be additions, possibly ones approved in 1872.

Incidental to the station building, but near the site, an interesting company minute of 1849 refers to the demolition of an observatory and that a company cottage was to be built with the materials.

The second station building was erected when Manton became an important junction with the opening of the Nottingham to Glendon Junction route for passengers in 1880. Two extra platforms were built on the new line (and the first two raised), all platforms being joined by a very long metal footbridge on substantial brick piers. The bridge was conveniently connected to a footpath

Manton Junction looking south-east showing the lines to Peterborough on the left and to Glendon Junction on the right. The original station building is in front of the tall grain store, the second station building centrally placed behind the long footbridge.

Manton's first station from the road side in 1985.

An early 1960s view of the unusual second station in the fork of the junction at Manton. (Neil Cossons)

on the west side of the site that linked the villages of Manton and Wing.

The second building is an oddly-shaped, single-storey structure at the fork of the junction, and is as plain as the first station was attractive. It comprises three parallel bays, tapered to suit the fork in which they stand, the roofs gabled at the southern end, but at the opposite end is an integral hipped-roof and the centre bay effectively extended and shaped to an unusual five-sided office. The original building was then solely used by the Station Master.

The layout of the platforms serving the lines to the south was changed as soon as 1886 when an extra line was added and a new platform built on the Down side. Substantial brick and timber waiting rooms were then provided on all platforms remote from the main building. Since closure these have disappeared with the platforms.

Services to Nottingham and London ceased from 18 April 1966 and those to Leicester and Peterborough from the following 6 June. In the end even the Uppingham residents could not be attracted to the station despite both its excellent service and extensive flower gardens which featured here.

LUFFENHAM

During the building of the Midland Railway's Syston & Peterborough line in 1847, the LNWR's Rugby & Stamford branch was being planned, and agreement reached for a junction of the lines near

Luffenham, just west of the station site. There was also agreement for the station to be jointly used from the opening of the LNWR line in 1851, although ownership was solely by the Midland. In the booking office there was a set of tickets held for each company, and both had their own booking hatches, in use until company grouping in 1923.

The elegant buildings were in limestone and completely symmetrical. The main two-storey house and booking office block was quoined, had pitched roof and skirted on ends and road side by narrow, single-storey bays. An open porch on the road side led to the booking office. Either side of the block, at right-angles, stood single-storey, pitched-roof buildings and between them along the platform side, ran a narrow verandah with single, sloping roof and deep valance. Windows were square-headed and all roofs had fish-scale slates. The deep valance was matched above the

Another variation in the diverse station designs on this line. This is Luffenham constructed in limestone.

A DMU bound for Stamford at Luffenham three months before the station's closure in 1966. (Andrew Muckley)

Variations of lamp design at Luffenham. (Neil Cossons)

opening of the small, timber shelter on the opposite platform.

The main building, situated east of the level crossing on the road running south-east from North Luffenham, was amply proportioned considering the small populations it served, even though it was a junction station. It remained practically unaltered, therefore, until closure in 1966. It was then turned to industrial use during which time the building generally deteriorated. Regrettably, this excellently-designed building was demolished in 1983 and the site is now used by a road transport company.

KETTON & COLLYWESTON

This splendid station was situated east of the crossing in Ketton on the Collyweston road and, like so many of the old buildings in the village, was constructed of local ironstone.

The main building had a slight Tudor appearance with raised gables and tall chimneys. It initially comprised a two-storey section which ran parallel to the platform, and, since enlargements of 1862, had two projecting bays centrally placed, two-storey to the rear and single-storey on the platform side. On the end wall of this latter section was a triangular bay window overlooking the platform, and a decorative bellcote which, as far as is known, never supported a bell. The end result was a building resembling a country school or chapel.

On the west side of the lower bay was the station entrance through a grand arched porchway, and on the east side was a short waiting room — at one time open-fronted. Further along the platform stood larger single-storey waiting rooms, which had been added in 1872 and also a lamp room of 1878.

Ketton & Collyweston in 1966 looking towards Leicester. (Andrew Muckley)

The view at Ketton & Collyweston looking in the opposite direction. (Andrew Muckley)

Detail of Ketton & Collyweston station house five years after closure. (R. Gulliver)

On the south-side platform a substantial shelter of stone was provided, part of which was open-fronted. Appropriately the roof on this and all buildings, were originally covered with the local Collyweston limestone 'slates'.

Indeed, the station name was changed in July 1935 from Ketton to Ketton & Collyweston by which it was known until the local services stopped in 1966. Demolition of buildings and platforms came seven years later.

LEICESTER & HITCHIN RAILWAY (MR)

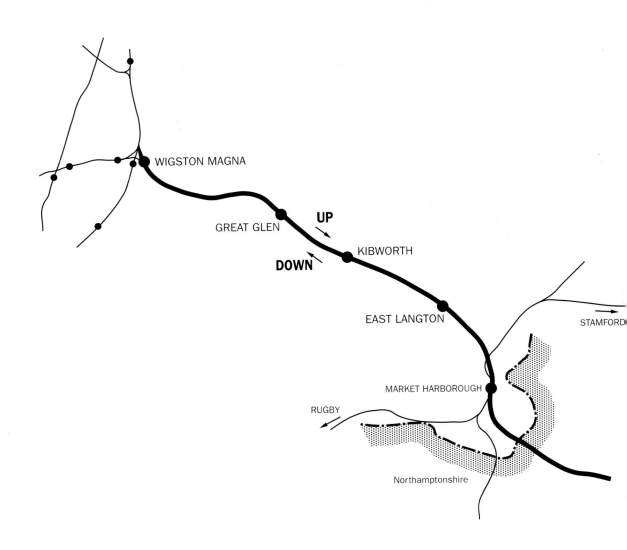

LEICESTER & HITCHIN RAILWAY (MR)

This was part of the Midland Railway's second main route to London, branching from Wigston southwards to join the Great Northern's main line at Hitchin. It opened for coal trains on 15 April 1857, and for passengers the following 8 May, although special celebratory trains had run the previous day.

In Leicestershire, three stations were opened with the line; at Wigston, Great Glen and Kibworth, whilst an existing station at Market Harborough was utilised, in collaboration with the London & North Western Railway, on a section that ran for a short distance over the Rugby & Stamford line (see Section 7).

The three original stations, combining station building and house, were similar and very distinctive. They were of a standard Victorian Gothic design by Charles Driver, with steeply-pitched roof on the rectangular, two-storey house, and all the station buildings featuring dentil decoration, and characteristic, elaborate bargeboarding complete with spiked finials. An angled, gabled porch made a pleasing entrance at the rear of the house. All buildings were in brick but the house wall on the platform side was rendered.

Windows were mostly in pairs, their headings round — Norman style — and in contrasting polychrome brick, some with embellished stone hoods. In the single-storey offices and waiting rooms, which were set at right angles to the house, windows also had attractive iron-lattice glazing. On the platform side of the offices was a waiting area, supporting ridge and furrow roofing, these County stations probably having three ridged sections originally, but from early photographs, the end one at Wigston appears to have been removed — or possibly never built.

Roofs of the waiting rooms on the opposite platform were in similar, ridged style, at least at Great Glen and Kibworth, and probably at Wigston, although here there is no definite evidence. It appears that with this design of roof there were intentions to add a compatible, ridged awning, but this was only carried out at the larger stations south of the County.

As detailed below, the three Leicestershire stations developed quite differently over the years, and there was an additional station, East Langton, built on the line north of Market Harborough that served the five Langton villages. Apparent from the traffic returns, the line proved popular with commuters, season ticket sales being high at all of the three original stations, although at Wigston Magna sales dropped inexplicably after the turn of the century.

Closure for local services within the County was from 1 January 1968, but freight and Inter-City trains continue to run to London, not, of course via Hitchin, since the Midland's own line to the Capital was completed in 1867:

WIGSTON MAGNA

Between South Wigston and Wigston Magna a short road passes in front of a public house, once the Railway Hotel but now called the 1852 Brewery Co. When the line was built, this road continued across the tracks on the level, the original station building just to the south on the Up side.

Towards the end of the 19th century, with freight traffic in particular being very heavy and with large sidings just to the north, the two tracks passing through the station and crossing became very restrictive. Re-modelling of the area became necessary, resulting in a bridge replacing the level crossing, two extra lines built outside each of the two platforms (which were retained and raised), and the station buildings replaced. A large Station Master's house was also erected north of the adjacent terrace of railway cottages on the north side of the road.

The west elevation of the original station at Wigston Magna taken shortly before replacement.

Possibly the Station Master's family posing in front of Wigston station around the turn of the century. (Note a lack of hood mouldings over the windows at this station.)

Typical of Midland Railway architecture at the beginning of the century displayed at Wigston Magna in 1952. (National Railway Museum)

Access to the new station was then from the top of the road bridge on the south side where, at this level, there was a substantial brick booking office, the base of which stood on the Down platform. It had features typical of Midland Railway buildings at this time. There were stone string courses and ball finials, terra-cotta mouldings announcing 'MR Wigston Station' over an iron-gated entrance, and raised stone-capped gables at front and rear, although two gables on the west side were plain.

The covered steps to the Down platform from the booking hall (with valance similar to those on the platform building) at Wigston Magna. (R. Gulliver)

Platform buildings at the second station at Wigston Magna, looking south in 1967. (R. Gulliver)

A glazed wooden entrance hall was cantilevered on the eastern side of this building and led passengers to a covered stairway for the Down platform, whilst a similar stairway led to the opposite platform from another iron-gated archway in the bridge. On each platform was a plain set of brick waiting rooms and usual facilities, both buildings with pitched roof and large, flat awnings, cantilevered and supporting a decorated valance.

The new station opened shortly after approval was given by the Board of Trade on 22 September 1902 and lasted, virtually unchanged, until closure of the line's stopping services in 1968.

An official announcement by the LMS changed the name of the station on 2 June 1924 from Wigston (L&H) to Wigston Magna, although the Midland and early LMS passenger timetables had only ever showed it as just Wigston (an exception was in the 1880s when the suffix 'Junction for

Birmingham' was added at the time when a through carriage from St Pancras was detached here for forwarding by local train to Birmingham via Nuneaton). In Midland minutes though, the station was normally referred to as Wigston (L&H), and in Bradshaws, for a few years before the turn of the century, it was listed as Wigston Junction.

All parts of the station have now been removed, leaving only the bricked-up entrances in the bridge to show any trace of its position. The Station Master's house lasted until replaced by a housing development in 1989, but the long row of railway cottages can still be seen.

GREAT GLEN

This station was not convenient for the village of Great Glen being situated some distance away on the opposite side of the main A6, one mile along the Fleckney road. The main building, still surviv-

A Down goods train passing Great Glen in 1948. (R. E. Tustin)

A 1984 road side view of Great Glen in use as business premises.

A Midland passenger train about to enter Great Glen where a grand rockery garden is displayed.

ing for residential and business purposes, lies east of the road on the Up side of the line. On this side only was there access from the road overbridge, so passengers had to make do with a board crossing to the opposite side.

There was very little alteration over the years to this standard design of station except for platform lengthening in 1862 and 1875. Also, the name was changed in January 1897 from Glen to Great Glen – the name generally adopted by the village having gradually changed from Glen Magna. One reason for changing, however, was probably to avoid confusion with Glen Parva.

Stations on the Leicester & Hitchin line varied in the colour of bricks used, and here they were white, although now blackened with age.

Due perhaps to its isolated position, closure came early, on 18 June 1951.

KIBWORTH

The main building, which was constructed on the site of an old rectory, can still be seen east of the road between Kibworth Harcourt and Kibworth Beauchamp. Unlike Wigston and Great Glen it was built on the Down side, but is a mirror image of those two, so waiting rooms are also on the south side of the house.

Alterations to the station have included lengthening of platforms in 1862 and 1870, and the provision of steps from the adjacent road overbridge to each platform in 1885. The following year, a footbridge was attached to the outside of the road-bridge wall to link the two flights of steps, and over 20 years later, the steps moved further apart to give more room on the platforms.

The booking office was extended in 1903, but during the 1950s the ridged-roof waiting area was gradually removed and replaced by a simple porch. Closure came when the local services stopped in 1968. This grand building, in white brick like Great Glen, was then converted for use as offices by a timber company. It remains substantially unaltered, still supporting some of the elaborate bargeboarding and lozenge-patterned windows.

A royal occasion at Kibworth in November 1907.
Princess Louise and the Duke of Argyll were
driven to the station after their visit to
Rolleston Hall.

Kibworth looking south. The goods shed, in polychrome brick, can still be seen as well as the main station building. (Stations U.K.)

The waiting rooms on the Up platform at Kibworth. The matching rooms attached to the main building had been removed when this photograph was taken in 1958. (Stations U.K.)

EAST LANGTON

On building the line, what was termed a market station was planned here, but was postponed, much to the annoyance of the locals who wrote to the company praying for access to the railway. Their pleas were not answered for nearly 20 years, however, until a station was opened on 2 October 1876. Built on an embankment, it was reached by a drive from the west side of the Church Langton to Market Harborough road.

The long, low main building, on the Up side, was of diagonal and vertical boarding with large hipped roof, overhung to form an awning with valance at ends and platform side. This was a similar but smaller version of the standard type of

East Langton in 1961 looking northwards. (Stations U.K.)

A class 9F heading towards Leicester through East Langton, about 1959. (J. C. Kirby)

Midland timber structure which could be seen at Grimston and Old Dalby (Section 6). Opening as Langton, it became East Langton from 1 May 1891.

In latter years, grounded van bodies, used for storage, stood at either end of the building, the one to the south replacing a lamp room. On the opposite platform, which was always reached by a rather dangerous board crossing across the main line, was a small, closed shelter with single sloping roof and boarding matching that of the main building.

Two cottages were provided in 1883 north of the station site, but neither, it appears, were for the Station Master. He had to wait until 1912 for a company house, when he was given one of a pair, built alongside the station approach road. Again, cessation of local services saw the end of the station in 1968, and just the houses and cottages remain.

DERBY AND ASHBY BRANCH
AND SAWLEY & WESTON LINE (MR)

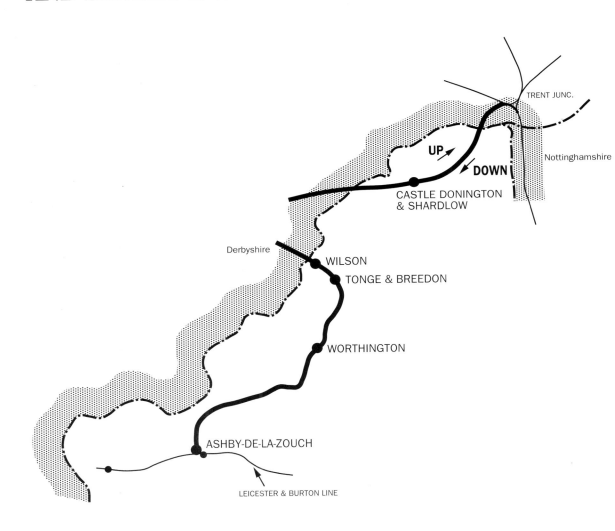

DERBY & ASHBY BRANCH
AND SAWLEY & WESTON LINE (MR)

The route from Derby to Ashby was opened in three stages. Firstly, the Melbourne Junction (on the Derby to Birmingham line) to Melbourne section was opened on 1 September 1868 for both goods and passengers, although at the time, the line stretched a further 1¼ miles to Tonge where an engine turntable was sited. The next section, to Worthington, opened for goods exactly a year later and for passengers on 1 October 1869.

This last, short extension appears to be an afterthought, as it necessitated the removal of the turntable to the new Worthington terminus where a temporary platform and shelter were required. Here the line, known as the Derby & Melbourne line, terminated for over four years until the final section, the Ashby & Breedon Line, was opened for all traffic on 1 January 1874. Again the turntable was moved, this time to the end of the line at Ashby.

The branch was single south of Melbourne and primarily built for mineral and agricultural traffic. There was certainly very little potential for passengers as only small villages were passed en route and this was reflected in the modest design of the four stations provided within the County.

Actually, there may have been a fifth station — at Lount — but of this there is some mystery. During construction of the line's last section in 1873, the planning committee were unsure whether a station, midway between Worthington and Ashby, would be viable. The order was made, therefore, for a temporary wooden platform with wooden booking shed to be provided (like Worthington) and a permanent station then built should traffic demand. It was to be sited at a point where the Heath End Colliery siding joined the main line, about ¼ mile south of Lount village west of the Ashby Road.

Despite this arrangement, the station never appeared in the Midland timetable after the branch opened, but there is further reference in company minutes of January 1875, stating that a station should be provided at Lount and that a plan should be submitted for approval. Whether this was to replace the temporary one, or the temporary one was cancelled and this was to be the first, is unknown, but there is no further reference in minutes, and again there is no entry in any Midland timetable. The assumption must be that the station was never built.

Little revenue would have been lost, however, because passenger traffic on the whole line was always very low and services were withdrawn as early as 22 September 1930.

Because the line was also little used for goods traffic it was one chosen for military training during the Second War. The section from Smisby Road, near Ashby, to Chellaston Junction was taken over by the War Department for use as the Melbourne Military Railway from 19 November 1939 and handed back to the LMS on the first day of 1945. Except for the first seven months, the occupiers agreed with the LMS to maintain the small amount of local goods and mineral traffic, and for a short time, at the start of their occupancy, they also ran a passenger service as far as Smisby Road.

Soon after the War came the line's first permanent closure. This was from Burton Road, Ashby to New Lount Colliery, effectively on 11 December 1949 with the closure of Ashby tunnel, followed by the remaining short section in Ashby at the southern end early in 1964. New Lount to Worthington closed completely from 27 November 1968 and traffic ceased on the remaining northern section from 21 May 1980.

Following the opening of the Derby & Melbourne line in 1868, a connecting branch was built, the Sawley and Weston line, from Chellaston Junction to Sheet Stores Junction at Trent. It opened for passengers on 6 December 1869 and for goods two weeks later.

A short section of it ran through Leicestershire on which one station stood, Castle Donington & Shardlow, to which reference is made at the end of this section. The line's passenger service ended in 1930 on the same day as the Derby & Ashby Branch, but this line remains open for freight services:

WILSON

This was barely within the County border, and situated east of the village on the south side of the main road. On the only platform here were the booking and waiting facilities contained in just one small brick structure with outbuilding at the north end. The main part was single-storey, rectangular in section, with hipped roof and round, stone-headed openings.

As it was not paying its way, perhaps because the stations on either side, Melbourne and Tonge, were both less than one mile away, it lasted for fewer than three years, and was closed from 1 June 1871.

In 1892 an order was given for the building to be converted into a platelayer's cottage, and thereafter it remained in remarkably good condition for this and other railway use until the 1960s. It then stood neglected for some time until, after much modification, it formed the basis of a modern-looking bungalow. Unfortunately its conversion has

Surviving an exceptionally long time after its early closure was Wilson, taken here from the south-west in 1972. (R. Gulliver)

Derelict Wilson from the platform side in the same year. (R. Gulliver)

Tonge & Breedon looking south, still in use as
a goods depot, about 1958.
(M. H. Billington)

An extra bay has been added
to Tonge & Breedon (and less
interesting windows) since
conversion for domestic use –
photographed in 1982.

hidden its appearance completely as a former station building.

TONGE & BREEDON

Although the line passed through the middle of Tonge village, the station was sited further to the north. It lay west of the line and on the north side of the A453 (before it was rerouted).

There was just one platform with a small station building identical to that at Wilson. A Station Master's house was provided a few months after the station opened, but to economise, was a conversion from the old village smithy, sited some distance from the station.

In May 1897 the station's name was changed from Tonge to Tonge and Breedon, and remained thus until closure with the line's passenger service in 1930. It stayed in railway use as a small goods yard remained on the site until 1959. There was also a goods storage shed on the platform. By the 1970s the main building was purchased for conversion into a private house and an extra bay added to the west side. Further alterations, however, have now hidden its railway identity.

WORTHINGTON

The building here was similar to Wilson and Tonge, but a few feet longer, and had an additional doorway on the track side. It was not situated on the single platform, however, but on the opposite, south side of the two lines that passed through here, the line nearer to it serving the Cloud Hill lime quarries.

All passengers crossed both tracks, therefore, to reach the platform, which could well have been the original, temporary one mentioned with the line's building as it was of timber, very low, and reference to building a new platform cannot be found in company minutes. On the platform was a timber shelter, open fronted and with single sloping roof.

Curiously, the station was built a long way from the more obvious location, next to the Breedon road. It meant that villagers had to walk across open fields directly north of the village to gain access. The large station house, though, built as late as 1907, was next to the road, where the line crossed by an overbridge.

After closure of the line for passengers, the station building remained in use for goods services until they ceased in 1964. Also used till this time was a plain, separate block of almost similar size that was erected west of the original building for use during the Second World War by the Military Railway. Both buildings were demolished around 1970, but the Station Master's house remains occupied.

Station building and shed erected during the Second War at Worthington in 1969 – looking south towards Ashby. (R. Gulliver)

Wooden platform and shelter at Worthington taken in 1949.
The Breedon and Cloud Hill Lime Works are in the distance.
(National Railway Museum)

A 1950s view of Ashby platform.
The line curved south-westerly
to join the Leicester-Burton
line in the distance.
(Lens of Sutton)

ASHBY-DE-LA-ZOUCH

This was situated where the branch joined the Leicester & Burton line on a north to west curve, with the junction facing away from the main Ashby-de-la-Zouch station. It seems odd at first that the curve was not built to allow trains from the branch into the main station, but as the branch trains always terminated here, it would have been necessary for a bay or further platform to be constructed at the principal station.

It was reasonable, therefore, to provide this separate, single platform, with run-round facilities at the end of the branch, although passengers were left with a long walk from the booking office at the main station. On the platform, built of stone (like Tonge and Wilson), a small waiting shed was provided.

Soon after grouping in 1923 the name of both stations was changed in timetables from Ashby to Ashby-de-la-Zouch. Sign boards were changed accordingly at the main station, but on the branch it was always Ashby.

The platform remained after the line's closure until houses completely covered the site in the 1970s.

CASTLE DONINGTON & SHARDLOW

East of the main road running north from Castle Donington village, the main building stood on the Down side of the line. It was very similar to Wilson, Tonge and Worthington, being single-storey with hipped roof, all openings round-headed and with an outbuilding at the eastern end.

Ashby platform, about 1961,
showing the newly-ballasted
freight line.
(Neil Cossons)

It was used more regularly than those it resembled though, for less than two years after opening it was lengthened by the addition of a large waiting room in matching style. On the opposite platform was a timber shelter with single sloping roof, also having round-headed openings.

In the hope of increasing its popularity, the station name was changed from Castle Donington to Castle Donington & Shardlow from May 1898 even though Shardlow was nearly two miles away. Nevertheless, passenger business was not popular enough, and services ceased from 22 September 1930.

After closure the station was used as a goods office and for occasional excursion trains which departed from here at least until 1960. The platforms were then removed, followed some years later by all buildings including the station house that was sited by the drive from the main road. The Station Master was fortunate here as the two-storey house was extremely roomy — being a conversion from an old inn.

Castle Donington & Shardlow looking towards Trent in 1952. (National Railway Museum)

The reverse view in 1965. (R. M. Casserley)

Castle Donington & Shardlow in 1969 from the road side. (R. Gulliver)

NOTTINGHAM & MELTON LINE (MR)

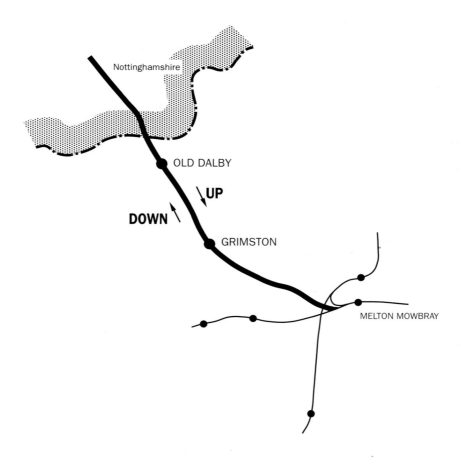

NOTTINGHAM & MELTON LINE (MR)

In addition to the Midland's main line to London, Nottingham was linked by an alternative route to the Capital that started on the Nottingham and Melton line and then ran south via a short part of the Syston & Peterborough line and Kettering. On the Nottingham & Melton section, traffic commenced for goods on 1 November 1879 and for passengers the following 2 February.

Only six miles of this line ran through Leicestershire where just two very similar stations were sited, Old Dalby and Grimston.

They, and the four stations in Nottinghamshire fared reasonably well initially, and in Midland days returned remarkably consistent passenger figures, although never particularly high and with little growth. However, during the 1930s and 40s traffic declined quite rapidly, such that by the late 1940s the stations over the County border were all closed, but the two Leicestershire stations survived longer as their individual details show.

Local services on the line ceased from 18 April 1966, and through passenger traffic to London discontinued from 1 May 1967. Through goods lasted until November the following year.

Most of the line, now single, remains in use as a vehicle test track between Melton Junction and the severed end at Edwalton, and at the southern end, coal has been moved over the line from a new super pit at Asfordby from early 1992:

OLD DALBY

This was situated directly east of the village where the large Station Master's house, independent of the station, still lies between the bridge carrying the line over the road and the station drive.

The main building, on the Up side, was of a fairly standard Midland pattern, very long and containing the usual facilities. It was completely of timber, with the walls above waist height of diagonal boarding. The slated, hipped roof over-hung on all four sides forming canopies that were given additional support by decorative iron brackets. The canopies were completed by a particularly ornate valance.

On the opposite platform the small shelter was of timber boarding matching the main building, but with just a single sloping roof.

The only early minuted alteration was in December 1886 when a stepway was sanctioned ascending the embankment from the road to the Up platform, although at some stage there had been a major alteration with the conversion of the

Typical Midland Railway style of timber buildings at Old Dalby in 1950, viewed in the Nottingham direction. (Stations U.K.)

Detail of the main building at Old Dalby.

Old Dalby in 1963.

platforms from timber to brick construction. Much later additions were small ancillary buildings situated at either end of the main structure.

In 1939 an Ordnance Depot was sited near the village, and along with its associated housing, brought added trade to the station. This, no doubt, helped its survival until closure of the Nottingham-Melton services from 18 April 1966.

Just the Up platform remains, the Down platform and station buildings being removed in about 1970. The Control Centre for the test track is now situated on the site.

GRIMSTON

This was actually in the hamlet of Saxelby after which it was intended to be named, but on opening, to distinguish it from Saxby (just east of Melton) it was changed to Grimston, a village a mile to the north of the station. Set in delightfully wooded surroundings, the station buildings, of practically the same design as Old Dalby, were reached by a long drive from the Saxelby direction. At the side of the drive the grand Station Master's house still stands.

The station was never as busy as Old Dalby, and with trade declining between the Wars, was put in control of the Old Dalby Station Master in about 1931. Fortunately this helped it survive longer than the Nottinghamshire stations (even though not as busy as some) and was not closed until 4 February 1957.

Little changed over the years, even oil lamps were used to the end. In 1956 the local council, hoping to stave off the threat of closure, attempted

*Very similar to Old Dalby
was Grimston, shown here
in 1970.
(R. Gulliver)*

*The view approaching
Grimston from the
east side.*

*A standard design
of Station Master's
house of the 1860s
and 70s at
Grimston,
taken 1989.*

to have the station converted to an unstaffed halt, and offered to construct a footpath from the Down platform to the road below, but without success. The Down platform and waiting shed were removed around 1970, but the main building was sold and used for storage, lingering for about 20 years before final removal. The Up platform survives as well as the station house.

RUGBY & STAMFORD BRANCH (LNWR)

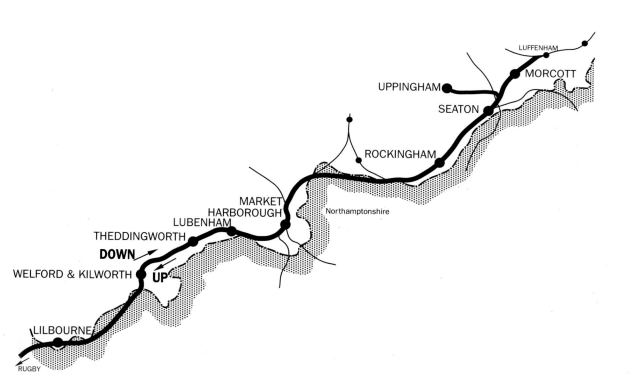

RUGBY & STAMFORD BRANCH (LNWR)

Much of this line ran along the Leicestershire / Northamptonshire border cris-crossing between the two counties but running mostly in the former. It was built in sections, the first just a single track from Rugby to Market Harborough that opened for goods on 29 March 1850. The first passenger trains were specials — for the directors' use on 27 April 1850 and for the Market Harborough fair two days later. Services proper started the following 1 May.

The remainder of the line was double track, the section to Rockingham opening for all traffic on 1 June 1850 and the final section, to the Junction at Luffenham on the Syston and Peterborough line — and hence completion of the through route from Rugby to Stamford — on 2 June 1851.

Like the Midland's Syston & Peterborough line it followed river valleys for most of its length on fairly flat land and crossed many roads on the level. In fact all stations were at road crossings except Lubenham and Market Harborough.

The stations planned for the line were all shown in the Construction Minutes for April 1847 and conveniently included their status thus:

Clifton (Warwicks.)	3rd class
Stanford (Northants.)	3rd class
Welford (Leics.)	2nd class
Theddingworth (Leics.)	3rd class
Lubenham (Leics.)	3rd class
Market Harborough (Leics.)	1st class
Weston (Northants.)	3rd class
Caldecott (Rutland)	Lodge
Seaton (Rutland)	Lodge
Luffenham (Rutland)	1st class

The last station listed was shown as a joint station with the Midland Railway, but later in 1847, when the Midland's Leicester & Hitchin line was authorised to run through Market Harborough, the two companies agreed that the Midland would

pay for building Luffenham, with the LNWR having free use, while the roles would be reversed at the Market Harborough station (with any differences in cost made up). This plan fell through, however, when the Midland's projected line was delayed for several years, but Luffenham was constructed by the Midland with occupancy by the LNWR. Curiously, in both companies' early minutes, this station is sometimes referred to as Morcott (where a station was built later) and could have originally been planned nearer to that village than to Luffenham.

There is a strong possibility that the design of the stations, some if not all, was the work of railway architect Sancton Wood. Despite his working on the Syston & Peterborough line at the time, the Construction Minutes show that he was paid £100 in October 1847, possibly for station design, but the precise reason is not revealed.

Sizes of the projected stations can be compared from their estimated costs: Market Harborough was £3250, Welford £2300 and the remaining seven, (all then classified as 3rd class) £750 each. In contrast were the many crossing-keeper's lodges on the line, 11 in all, estimated at £180 each. By the time of construction though, director Edward Watkin (later Chairman of the Great Central Railway) reported that despite the lodges being two-storey, their cost had been reduced to £150. Many of the lodges can still be seen. They are mostly east of Market Harborough and like the stations on this section are of limestone construction.

In addition to the planned stations, sites were seriously considered at Lyddington, Husbands Bosworth, Morcott and Lilbourne, but only the last two were eventually built despite many requests in subsequent years for facilities at Husbands Bosworth.

In 1868 platforms at all the stations, except Market Harborough, were ordered to be raised to

3'-0" high — not for the passengers' convenience but to ease the unloading of the many hunting horses used in these parts. Market Harborough had separate facilities.

Partly in preparation for the traffic expected from the projected Seaton to Peterborough branch via Wansford (opened 21 July 1879), the line between Rugby and Market Harborough was doubled during 1878. Stations were affected by the widening with the provision of extra platforms and some new buildings. Work progressed so well that by November it was reported that the waiting rooms were nearly finished, 'wanting only a little papering'! The completed works were passed for use on 11 January 1879.

The new buildings were in the LNWR's new modular type of construction. They were of varying sizes, all in horizontal timber boarding and with flat roof that projected to form awnings on three sides. The largest projections over the platforms were supported by large, ornate brackets of cast iron and a very decorative design of valance was used at all stations. Some valances over the platform edge were eventually reduced for clearance purposes when the large awnings started to sag with age.

These typical LNWR buildings remained a feature of the line until the line's closure with all stations, except Market Harborough (see station text for reason) from 6 June 1966. Goods trains had ceased from the previous 6 April.

In this section, Uppingham is included, the only station on the short, single-line branch that ran from Seaton:

LILBOURNE

Lilbourne village is in Northamptonshire but the station lay just within the County border on the level

The crossing-keeper's house at Lilbourne – probably adapted for use as a booking office when the station first opened.

Lilbourne in 1966 looking towards Rugby.
(Andrew Muckley)

Lilbourne showing timber signal box attached to the main building.
The M1 motorway was being constructed when this photograph was taken in 1963.

with the Catthorpe road. It was not planned with the line but villagers, including clergy, pressed regularly for a station soon after the line opened, and following experiments with stopping trains a regular service started on 1 November 1854.

A crude, single platform was provided east of the level crossing and was subsequently made permanent in 1860. On the opposite side of the road can still be seen the original two-storey, crossing-keeper's house that most likely served as the station booking office until a proper office with waiting room was provided on the platform in 1870. Had the house been used for booking, it may explain the very early extension which can still be detected at the end of the building.

With the 1878 track doubling two new platforms with standard timber structures were provided, the main building on the Up side, whilst opposite was an open-fronted shelter. At the western end of the main building was attached the station signal

box, constructed similarly to the station in horizontal timber boarding.

All this may have changed though due to an unusual request made in 1909 by the owner of nearby Catthorpe Towers. He asked for the whole station to be moved 600 yards nearer to Rugby to allow the road to be re-routed away from his residence. When he was presented with the exorbitant cost this would incur (sum undisclosed) the idea was soon forgotten.

In January 1965 the station became 'partly staffed' for the last seven months of its life and since closure the wooden buildings have been removed. Platforms and a lamp room survive in addition to the original crossing house which remains occupied.

WELFORD & KILWORTH

The station was situated on the south side of the A427 road between North Kilworth (1/2 mile dis-

The line runs north in the Stamford direction through Welford & Kilworth, seen here about 1960.

On the north side of the level crossing at Welford & Kilworth was a United Dairies depot where these milk churns were probably destined. The hut between the platform shelter and signal box was a second booking office. (Stations U.K.)

The station entrance, crossing-keeper's cottage and very tall signal box at Welford & Kilworth in 1966. (R. Gulliver)

tant) and Husbands Bosworth (1½ miles distant); so it is surprising that when the station opened it was called Welford, a village smaller than the other two and 3¼ miles away.

From 1853 though, it was entitled Welford, Kilworth, two years later, Welford & Kilworth, and in 1897, Welford & Lutterworth. This last change was probably due to competition from the impending Great Central station in Lutterworth, despite it being 5½ miles away. (The change would not have been necessary had Lutterworth residents achieved success with their petitioning in 1861 for a branch from the Rugby & Stamford line to their own town, starting from Clifton Bridge.) 1913 saw a reversion to the final name, Welford & Kilworth.

The main buildings, on the Up side, comprised the Station Master's house of 1½ storeys running parallel to the line with station offices attached at the platform side. These were basically two, sin-gle-storey blocks set at right-angles, the north one projecting onto the platform, with square bay window in the end wall. All roofs were steeply pitched including that on a large timber porchway, an attractive feature that led to the station offices on the road side.

In order that only one gatekeeper need be employed a cottage was erected for his use in 1861 facing the station at the end of the Down platform. It was a sizeable, two-storey building with dormer windows and although termed a cottage was actually larger than the station house.

An enlargement was carried out though, to the station house in 1881, with an extension to both storeys, enabling the parlour to be used as a waiting room. There followed in 1896 a conversion of the booking office into a parcels and left luggage office, whilst the ladies waiting room was adapted for the issue of tickets. The ladies then had to make do with a standard wooden hut sited alongside the station buildings. There was also a single-storey extension on the east side of the house.

On the Down side the open platform shelter was in the 1878 timber style prevalent on the line, and on the same platform an extra hut was provided in 1903 for use as a waiting room and extra booking office. How long it lasted is unknown. Next to the road on this side was a large LNWR signal box standing on an immensely tall brick base to give a clear view of the line above the adjacent gate-keeper's house.

Little happened at the station until 1965 when the platforms were renovated and a new array of British Railways' concrete lamp posts were installed. This was all rather late as the station closed with the line's passenger service just over a

year later. All buildings survived for about ten years before demolition, but the timber shelter remained until 1987 when this last remnant of the station was moved to the Coventry Steam Railway Centre for preservation. A company hiring portable buildings now occupies the site.

THEDDINGWORTH

The station buildings can still be seen next to where the line crossed the narrow lane to Laughton north of the village. The simple main building, which contained the station house with small booking office and waiting room, comprised originally of two, two-storey bays in 'T' formation with pitched roofs and the small-paned windows square-headed. Since private ownership there have been single-storey additions at front and rear and brickwork rendering.

Theddingworth viewed towards Rugby in 1966. (Andrew Muckley)

The main building at Theddingworth. The station name was displayed in large letters between upper & lower floors of the right-hand bay. (R.Gulliver)

A feature sometimes used by the LNWR was the displaying of the station name in large letters high on the house wall (continental style). It was used at Theddingworth on the cross bay overlooking the platform, but as it was painted on it became barely discernible in later years. (Some LNWR stations used painted boards at the same elevation instead.)

On the opposite platform, appearing completely intact, remains the waiting shelter of the standard, flat roof design provided on the line's 1878 doubling. It was a large affair considering the small population served and contained separate waiting rooms. At the end of the same platform by the crossing, the station signal box also survives (externally at least) and unusual in that the top half was rebuilt with flat roof after a fire.

The population of Theddingworth varied very little during the time the station was open (only between two and three hundred) and with no other village nearby feeding the station there was no necessity for significant alterations except for the addition of a pre-cast concrete lamp room. Despite the low usage, the station survived until the closure of local services in 1966. The house soon became quite derelict, but has since been transformed into a very attractive residence. The platform shelter and signal box are now used as domestic outbuildings.

LUBENHAM

The station was planned with the line, but for economic reasons was not opened until 1 September 1869 and then only after years of petitioning by

The Station Master's house at Lubenham in 1984, probably also used as a booking office when the station opened. The building attached at the rear was the signalman's house.

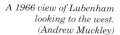

A 1966 view of Lubenham looking to the west. (Andrew Muckley)

Detail of the open platform shelter at Lubenham in 1970. (R.Gulliver)

local residents. The platform was sited on an embankment south of the village, west of a bridge that spanned the A427. A shelter was provided on the platform in 1872.

A short distance to the south, a pair of attached, two-storey houses were built for the Station Master and signalman. In the larger, Station Master's house, built facing the line, there is evidence from the layout of the rooms that this building originally contained the booking office although its position would have been rather inconvenient to residents of Lubenham, being on the side of line furthest from the village.

With the 1878 track widening the booking office was better sited on the north platform, reached by an inclined path ascending the embankment from the road. The building also contained waiting rooms and was of the LNWR's standard flat roof variety, as was the new open shelter on the Up platform. Incidentally, the few passengers that arrived from the south of the station for departure from the this platform had to make their way through the small goods yard. This was very often crammed with cattle received from Ireland for fattening on the area's rich pastures.

In 1882 a brick lamp room was provided behind the Down platform and a 'portable' hut added at the eastern end of the same platform some time later. All was removed from the station site after closure of the passenger service in 1966, but the two houses remain occupied, the ex-Station Master's having, from 1996, a large annex at the front.

MARKET HARBOROUGH

Because the current station is on the main line to London, it is easily assumed that this has always

Market Harborough's first station, taken about 1880, showing its northern elevation facing Bowden Road. The goods shed and hotel cabs can be seen.

been so. However, the first station on the site was on the Rugby & Stamford line and it was only because the Midland's Leicester & Hitchin line, built seven years later, utilised a short section of the Rugby & Stamford line through Market Harborough, that the station became a stop on the London route. When the Midland arrived they rented sections of the station from the LNWR.

The original site had a conventional two-platform layout with the main building on the Down side, reached from the Great Bowden Road by a drive on the south side of St. Mary's churchyard. The platforms were positioned only a short distance to the north-west of those in use today.

The main building consisted of two, parallel, pitched-roof bays, end on to the platform, the one to the south longer and of one-and-a-half storeys (presumably the Station Master's quarters) whilst the other was single storey. They were joined by a short, pitched-roof section, on the road side of which was attached an entrance hall with flat, projecting canopy (a late addition).

The buildings were completed by a long, single-storey bay running northwards from the side of the lower bay, with a pitched-roof verandah on the platform side supported on wooden pillars. Windows were elaborate; square-headed with lozenge pattern designs, some had shades supported by short, decorative brackets, whilst others were quoined. Tall angular chimneys added to the station's excellent design.

Alterations and additions were frequent, not only due to the Midland sharing the station but also because of other increases in traffic. As well as the exchange of passengers from one company's line to another there was extra business from the LNWR's branch from Northampton (1859), from their joint line with the Great Northern to Nottingham which branched from Welham Junction east of Market Harborough (1879) and also as a result of the Midland's many extensions to their main line.

As early as 1866 the LNWR were considering radically enlarging the station to prevent the Midland building their own in the town and 'thereby missing out on the large tolls that the Midland paid', but it was some years later that the accommodation problem was finally resolved. Arrangements were made for a new joint station to be built, owned and run equally by both companies, although the LNWR were responsible for the design under their engineer Francis Stevenson.

The new station, the existing one, was opened on 14 September 1884 and laid out in the 'V' formed by the two companies' lines which converged from the south. In the new layout the lines of each company were kept quite separate through the platforms. The overall plan of the station was fairly symmetrical, although on the LNWR side, the west, there were extra bay platforms, one at the south for local Northampton trains, and one at the opposite end for Nottingham trains via Melton Mowbray.

All platforms were at high level with the main station building central in the 'V' at ground level and fronted by a large forecourt. The building is two-storey and has a design that is both individ-

A platform view of the first station at Market Harborough. The tracks in the distance curve to the right for Rugby and to the left for London.

The second station at Market Harborough from the south in 1965. The line to London is on the right.

ual and grand. Described as Queen Anne style, it is quite in keeping with other Georgian architecture in the town. It features stone pilasters, moulded door and window casings and central dormer window in the hipped roof. Tall chimneys are prevalent (some were removed for several years but have now been rebuilt). Over the main entrance is a glazed, cantilevered awning of three ridged sections with hipped ends that blends well with the building design.

The booking hall is central on the ground floor with station offices on either side (originally including ones for separate Station Masters) whilst upstairs there is living accommodation. From the booking hall passengers reached the outer platforms via subways and steps, but for the central, island platform a long inclined approach was provided, covered with pitched roof and glazed on either side.

Once a lamp room and porters rooms stood close to the point where the island platform is reached and facing the incline was the bookstall. Behind this stretched a large array of ordinary, typical

Awning detail at Market Harborough.

A view from the booking hall. The passage to the left led to the platforms for Rugby, Stamford, Northampton and Melton.

Platform buildings at Market Harborough, typical of large LNWR stations. The view is looking north in 1966 and canopies are being removed. (Andrew Muckley)

LNWR brick waiting rooms which were repeated on the outer platforms. All had flat roofs which extended to form a vast amount of awning area covering all platforms, and supported by rows of plain iron columns. The valances were also with little embellishment — if they had, the overall plainness apparent on this side of the station would surely have been avoided. The many skylights in the awnings though, helped brighten the platforms.

Thus the station remained with few alterations until passenger services started to decline. It was the former LNWR services which were to suffer most; those on the Joint Line closing in 1953, to Northampton in 1960 and on the Rugby & Stamford line in 1966. With the last closure the LNWR platforms were redundant and all buildings on the west side demolished whilst the awnings on the other platforms were severely shortened to reduce maintenance costs. At the same time the remaining buildings were refurbished and the ticket office, once divided between LNWR and MR, moved from the foot of the inclined approach to its current position inside the booking hall.

Only 11 years later, during 1977-8, all platform buildings were razed and replaced by the more manageable, brick waiting rooms seen today. Noticeable is the placing of the Down-side building well back from the platform edge in anticipation of one day straightening the severe curve through the station. During work on the platform the main two-storey building was again renovated and is now a Grade II listed building.

Modern platform buildings at Market Harborough, 1982.

Other recent work includes extension of the Down platform in 1986 and 1990, and provision of a large carpark alongside the station where the LNWR platforms once stood. These alterations are partly the result of the station becoming popular with regular commuter traffic to London using high-speed trains.

ROCKINGHAM

The station was built very close to the village of Caldecott by which name it was known during its construction. On opening, however, it was named after the smaller, but more renowned (because of the castle) village of Rockingham which was one mile to the south and over the County border in Northamptonshire.

The station building can still be seen west of the Caldecott to Rockingham road and is much larger than the small lodge station originally planned. It appears that a bay was added at some stage —

maybe an extension approved only four months after opening which is the only large alteration mentioned in company minutes. One alteration not mentioned is the addition of two semi-dormer windows, which, almost certainly, are not original. The building is essentially two-storey, T-section in plan like Theddingworth, with the additional bay to the rear — but the special difference here is that it is of limestone construction rather than brick. (Also similar in plan were two other stations on the line — but over the County border — at Yelvertoft & Stamford Park which was brick and Ashley & Weston in limestone.) Like Theddingworth, the station name was painted in large letters high on the station wall and this is still visible today.

During its first year a horse bus ran between the station and Uppingham town, but this lasted only until the more convenient station for Uppingham was opened at Seaton. In 1878 the platforms were

Rockingham in 1952 looking towards Stamford. (National Railway Museum)

The limestone main building at Rockingham, 1983.

lengthened and in the following year the station signal cabin erected by the level crossing opposite the main building. On the same side and still there since the station closed in 1966, is a small, timber waiting shelter, a closed type with single sloping roof, its rear supported on brick piers.

SEATON

This opened as a small country station between the villages of Seaton and Harringworth, but more importantly served the town of Uppingham, nearly three miles distant. Connecting the town and station was a regular horse-bus service, which became particularly busy when pupils were fer-ried to and from the large public school in Uppingham at the beginning and end of each term. In fact it was because of the headmaster at the school that the station changed its name from Seaton to Seaton & Uppingham, on his request, in October 1860.

Because of major alterations during its life the station's early appearance is uncertain, but from a small enclosure plan of 1856, it appears there were two bays at right angles and an outbuilding, similar in lay-out to Theddingworth. It was probably in local limestone and of two storeys like the crossing lodges which remain in the area. After

Seaton in 1966 facing Rugby.
The diesel unit in the bay platform
is bound for Stamford.
(Andrew Muckley)

A notice at Seaton which had
no relevance when taken in 1961.
(Neil Cossons)

Down-side buildings at Seaton.
(Neil Cossons)

some minor enlargements in 1860 more radical changes occurred in 1878 in preparation for its new status as a junction station the following year. (The junction was for the new, shorter line to Peterborough which branched just east of the station.)

Principally, the changes involved moving the offices, booking hall etc away from the station house to a new, lengthy timber building stretching eastward from the house. The new structure was in typical LNWR style of horizontal rusticated boarding, but there were differences to the stan-

dard of the time. Instead of one separate, protruding canopy there was a large hipped roof which overhung to form canopies on both platform and road sides. The casement windows, rather than sash were also different to standard.

It is believed to have been at the same time that the house buildings were also radically altered and the unusual arrangement of single-storey bays added at the west side. These extra buildings matched what is assumed to be the original section with their limestone construction and similarly pitched roofs.

Main building detail at Seaton a few days before the line's 1966 closure – hence the weeds in the track (B.J.Smith)

A road side view of Seaton, 1983. The flat-roofed section is a modern addition.

Another change was the addition of two bay platforms, both facing towards Stamford, and situated on the outside of the two existing platforms. The one on the Up side was mainly used for goods, but the other was for the local push-pull services to Stamford, necessary as there were fewer trains on this line when the new Peterborough route of 1879 opened. In connection with the new layout, a ground frame (operational when released by the junction signal box) was sited at the crossing end of the Down platform.

There followed in 1880 provision of a lamp room and brick crossing-keeper's hut on the Down side. The crossing gates, it seems, would normally be left closed to road traffic as a large bell was provided with a notice informing road users to ring for the porter whenever the gates required opening. It shows how busy the line was compared with the road.

In 1893 a footbridge was provided by the crossing necessitating part of the stone building to be removed to accommodate the bridge steps on the Up side. The new bridge was part of the preparation, along with other alterations the following year, for a service on the new, short branch to Uppingham that curved away about half-a-mile east of the station. This service was opened to passengers in October 1894 and at the same time the station title became just Seaton again. The Uppingham train always started, like the Stamford one, from the Down bay platform although on occasions would arrive at the bay on the opposite side.

This branch service was to last until 13 June 1960, but all trains were stopped when the main line closed six years later. During its last few

months the station had some claim to fame when it saw the last steam push-pull service in the country. The final run was to Stamford on 2 October 1965 when diesel units took over.

Of the closed stations remaining in Leicestershire this one is probably the most complete; still to be seen are the stone and timber main buildings, platforms, closed timber waiting shelter on the Down side, crossing-keeper's hut and the footbridge. The main buildings, with modern additions, are now used as residential and office accommodation by the owners of the site which is currently used for car breaking.

MORCOTT

Residents of Morcott had seen trains passing through their village for nearly 50 years before they were to have a station of their own. They had campaigned for railway access on several occasions, ever since the line was proposed, but were not rewarded until 31 October 1898. Even then it was only after a very generous offer from a Mr. Rowley, the local squire, who gave part of his land, and also local farmers offering assistance with building the approach road, that finally enticed the LNWR into allowing a station to be built.

One condition on which Mr. Rowley parted with his land was that the station should be open for at least five years. This it was and actually continued in use right up to closure in 1966. Throughout this time services were provided by the local push-pull train that plied between Seaton and Stamford.

The small station was north of the village, the approach road leading off High Street, and station

111

Morcott from the south in 1966.
(Andrew Muckley)

offices situated on the Down side of the line. Facilities were contained in a long, modular building of timber, with pitched roof — typically LNWR — but the normal canopy was not provided, only small covers over the doorways leading onto the platform. For reasons of cost both platforms were of timber, linked halfway along by a metal footbridge. A small shelter was provided on the Up side.

The two platforms were not used for long, however, for the line was singled completely between Seaton Junction and Luffenham by 21 July 1907, and the Up platform and bridge removed. Also to go was the signal box, situated at the east end of the Down platform since 1901, and replaced by a ground frame to operate the small goods yard.

With the exception of siting a 'portable' hut at the east end of the main building, little was to happen at the station until it became an unstaffed halt approximately three years before closure with the line. Now, all structures have been removed with the exception of a weighbridge office, and the site occupied by a timber company.

UPPINGHAM

This was another station opened because of continual pressure from residents, beginning with a petition raised during the planning of the Rugby & Stamford line in the hope that the railway would pass near the town. This failed — as did other attempts over the years to encourage either the Midland or LNWR to build a branch into the town from their own main lines — but eventually

Looking towards the buffer stops at Uppingham a year after its 1960 closure to passengers.
(A.G.Ellis)

the latter did capitulate. The Company would only pay for construction, though, and agreement was reached for landlords and various benefactors of the area to provide or purchase all the necessary land. Instrumental at the start of negotiations was the head of the large public school in Uppingham, Edward Thring, although he died before the start of construction.

The three-mile, single-line branch was built from Seaton and terminated in Uppingham in the south-east corner of the town. Facilities were open for goods on 17 September 1894 and for passengers on the following 1 October, although specials for the school had run into the station four days before this. It was by an agreement with the school that these specials always ran at the beginning and end of each term, with through coaches to and from various parts of England. This was despite more convenient trains being available at Manton and Seaton, the two stations hitherto used by Uppingham residents.

At this smart country station a single platform was provided (though unnecessarily long) with run-round facilities. The building, also extensive, was a characteristically LNWR structure of rustic, horizontal boarding with hipped roof. A flat, cantilevered canopy on rather plain brackets extended over the platform and at both ends of the building — the extension particularly large at the western end to cover the passenger entrance. A ridged skylight ran the length of the canopy and the valance was deep with a simple saw-tooth edge.

At the Seaton end of the building an open lever frame was situated on the platform (an LNWR trait) whilst at the opposite end was the brick, two-storey Station Master's house facing the station at right angles, and although large, was of simple design.

There were no notable alterations recorded in company minutes suggesting that the station was always adequate for its needs — in fact it was probably always larger than required. Passenger services ceased from 13 June 1960, whilst the last school special ran after the 1963 Christmas vacation. Goods traffic was terminated from 1 June 1964 since when the station and house have been removed and the site gradually taken over by industrial units.

The station house and rear of Uppingham station still in excellent repair in 1961.
(A.G.Ellis)

SOUTH LEICESTERSHIRE
RAILWAY

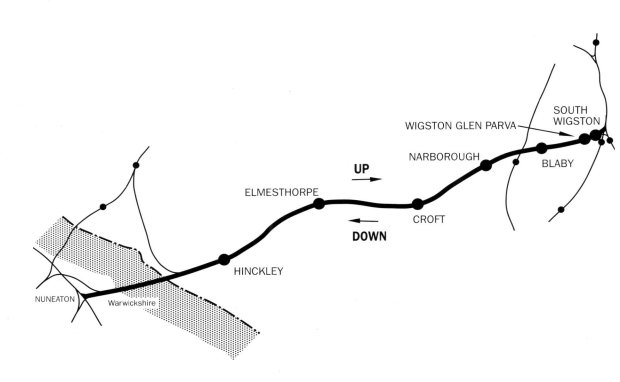

SOUTH LEICESTERSHIRE RAILWAY

This began as the Nuneaton & Hinckley Railway which was formed to construct a short line between the two towns, but in 1860, with the company having broader aspirations, the name was changed to the South Leicestershire Railway. Initially though, the line ran for just three miles between the existing Nuneaton station on the LNWR's Trent Valley line and Hinckley, opening as a single line on 1 January 1862.

From the outset the line was run by the LNWR under whose guidance it continued, still single, to join the Midland Railway's main line at Wigston. This section opened for passengers exactly two years to the day after the first and for goods on 1 February 1864. The LNWR took over the South Leicestershire Company officially in 1867 at a time when the track was being doubled, an operation completed by January 1868.

Unusual, was the line's direction nomenclature. Contrary to normal LNWR practice where the Up direction on cross-country lines always pointed towards their own main line, here it was towards the Midland line at Wigston — probably a result of the LNWR not being the original owners.

Beyond Hinckley the original intention was to build three stations — at Elmesthorpe, Narborough and Whetstone — for which the line's engineer John Addison prepared a standard design of building. However, because of the LNWR's growing financial problems at the time it was decided to build only temporary facilities at Narborough and Whetstone. Plans were then soon changed again because Whetstone (proposed for a site north of the village where the line still crosses beneath Enderby Road) was considered to be too near Narborough and was shelved. This did allow for the provision of a small station on the high embankment at Blaby and for the standard design of station to be used at Narborough. It was reported that Whetstone would be built later if traffic demanded, but this never transpired.

The amount of traffic expected at the stations is reflected in the initial staffing arrangements. These were: three porters and a Station Master at Elmesthorpe; a chief clerk, four porters and a gatekeeper at Narborough; and at Blaby, just one porter — although here there was no goods traffic to handle.

At all the stations, except Hinckley, it appears that waiting sheds were not considered in the plans as complaints poured in after the line opened requesting their provision. It was not for several years later that they were supplied.

On this line the Midland Railway had running rights, but they made little use of the stations; Hinckley, however, was always in their timetable. The other stations were used by the Midland only until 1869, with exceptions at Elmesthorpe, where conditional stops were made by a few trains from 1896 until the 1923 grouping, and at Wigston Glen Parva — one of two additional stations on the line — where just one Midland train stopped each way between October 1917 and grouping. The other additional station was at Croft.

All the stations, except Hinckley, were to close on the same day, when local services were withdrawn from 4 March 1968. The line is still active and Narborough has reopened, followed by a new station at South Wigston:

HINCKLEY

Originally the station was set in open fields south of the town, reached only by a track directly from the market place, although gradually new access roads were built. It may have been because the station was a long way from the town centre, or just for financial reasons, but the building provided for a town of Hinckley's standing was unjustifiably plain and undistinguished.

The main, pitched-roof buildings still comprise the narrow, former Station Master's house of 2½

115

Hinckley from the road side
in 1952.
(National Railway Museum)

*Army volunteers on the Down
platform at Hinckley at an
unknown date. They are
probably off to their annual
summer training camp or to
more serious matters in
France before 1918.
(Leicestershire Libraries)*

storeys and parallel single-storey bay that once contained the waiting rooms. Between the two runs a short single-storey section in which were the station offices and entrance hall, one office having a bay window on the platform side. Originally this linking section formed a recess on the road side, but was eliminated in 1897 with a well-blended extension which stood proud of the main block. To this was added a cantilevered awning, originally glass covered.

Also in 1897 sizable waiting rooms were built in brick on the Down platform and awnings added to this and the main buildings. The awnings were large affairs of corrugated iron curving away from the building and supported by cantilevered brackets. The larger awning, which remains on the main building, is also upheld by four wooden pillars along the centre of the platform. In the same period, platforms were extended and a metal footbridge provided at the western end, curved corrugated iron sheets again used to form a roof over steps and bridge. From the station's earliest days the platforms were also spanned at the opposite end by a public footbridge of metal on brick piers (the original station plans actually show a subway) the stout piers also doubling as store rooms. Both bridges were close to the main building and because of this and the presence of large awnings, the platform side of the station had an oppressive feel that lasted until recent alterations.

Other buildings provided were two wooden offices for a Station Master and porter situated by the public bridge on the Up side. It is possible they were originally for sole use by the Midland Railway who had employed their own staff at the station since 1868. From this date the Midland also had a booking window separate from the LNWR, in use until the LMS days of 1923. In revenue terms, the Midland probably fared as well at Hinckley as the LNWR, with only their trains serving the important route to Birmingham as well as having their share of the Leicester traffic.

Major rebuilding of the platforms occurred in 1924 and the Up side awnings extended westwards in 1933. That was the main extent of alterations until 1972 when, supposedly to save maintenance costs, the large block of waiting rooms on the Down platform was removed and replaced by an incongruous, bus-stop type shelter. In 1977 the public footbridge was renewed and the adjacent wooden offices removed at the same time.

That which remained was redeveloped between 1987 and 1990. The house was altered and its outbuildings replaced to form private offices for letting. The footbridge at the western end of the station was removed (then without covering which had blown off in a gale before the Second War) and the public bridge utilised to gain access to the platforms.

More private offices were provided at the western end, partly comprising a new single-storey block, and partly the old main waiting rooms and entrance hall. Lastly, the main offices were converted to form a new booking office and modern booking hall-cum-waiting room, the layout of which has, coincidentally, reverted to that of 1862. The external entrance is now covered with a new pitched-roof porch matching the entrance to the new private offices, the original awning having been removed.

Hinckley in 1952 - looking towards Leicester. (Lens of Sutton)

Platform detail at Hinckley in 1990. This remaining part of the canopy is the original section.

With these modern improvements the station's future seems more secure especially as it now stands in a developed area and no longer in open fields.

ELMESTHORPE

The station was close to diminutive Elmesthorpe, but it particularly served the larger villages of Barwell, Earl Shilton and Stoney Stanton. Indeed the station was suffixed 'for Barwell and Earl Shilton', but not until February 1904. Stoney Stanton missed out on the title despite it being nearest by half-a-mile. The station was west of the road to this latter village with the main buildings on the Down platform.

The rather austere buildings included the Station Master's house that comprised a pair of attached, two-storey bays at right-angles to the platform, the west bay narrower and only one room deep. The ground floor of this latter bay was

originally used as a porter's room. On the east side, running along the platform, adjoined the single-storey waiting rooms and booking facilities, one office having a small triangular bay window giving a limited view along the platform. This office eventually became part of the booking hall. All roofs were pitched except for a hipped portion at the end of the single-storey bay.

An improvement over the dull main buildings was the traditional LNWR shelter of horizontal boarding on the opposite platform. It was a large affair with flat roof projecting right to the platform edge and supporting a shapely valance. The shelter was provided in 1880 and later, either side of it, timber sheds were added. One was for storage and the other originally served as a second booking office, provided on this side of the line as it was more convenient for the larger villages mentioned, and also on the side of the most popular trains — those to Leicester.

Looking towards Leicester from Elmesthorpe station. Tickets were obtainable from both platforms.

Elmesthorpe in 1968. The necessity for portable steps at the low platform can be seen. (Andrew Muckley)

LNWR timber buildings in evidence at Croft, February 1968. (Andrew Muckley)

A Leicester to Birmingham DMU calling at Croft on the same day in 1968. (Andrew Muckley)

In the 1890s steps were provided to each platform from the road overbridge thus eliminating a boarded crossing, whilst portable steps were used here until closure to assist the less able passengers in and out of the carriages as the platforms were always low. On the Up platform was the station signal box at the western end, whilst opposite was a high water tank for which the platform had been extended in 1894.

After the 1968 closure the station area became a car breaker's yard and although the timber buildings were quickly removed, the main buildings lasted, quite derelict, until about 1980.

CROFT

The line passes just south of Croft village but a station was not provided until almost 14 years after the line's opening. So keen were the villagers to have a station, 'a Mr Pochin and other locally' contributed approximately one fifth towards its cost of £1209, and the station opened on 1 December 1877.

This was the time when the LNWR were introducing their modular timber style of buildings and these were used for the main structure on the Up side and the opposite platform shelter. Buildings were similar to those on the Rugby and Stamford line, but here the canopies formed by the large,

119

flat roofs extended only on the platform side. Also, a series of simple timber braces was used to support the awning rather than the later LNWR's standard ornate brackets.

As well as from the main driveway, the platforms could be reached by footpaths from the adjacent road overbridge. In about 1950 the path to the Down platform was removed, but steps always led to this platform from the adjacent Arbor Road.

The first alteration was approved in 1885 for the making of a goods office by extending the west side of the booking office. Matching timber was not used, but concrete slabs, appropriately a product of the local Croft Granite Company. In 1892 the Station Master was provided with a company house, built alongside company cottages on the west side of Station Road.

The platforms, faced with local granite, were lengthened in 1904 and in 1922 extra office accommodation was again required. For this an LNWR 'portable' wooden office was transferred from Blaby — maybe one temporarily used there during the long delay in rebuilding the burnt-out station.

Croft was for many years a very well tended station with prize-winning gardens, but all disappeared on its closure in 1968. Soon after, the buildings were burnt down. Now, only the Station Master's house and cottages remain.

NARBOROUGH

Even though the buildings here are plain, at least they have survived, mostly as originally built and still used for their intended purpose. The line's standard station design was used, although with Whetstone not being built, this applied only to Elmesthorpe, previously described, and Narborough, both of which were identical but on opposite sides of the track. The station is near the centre of the village on the level with the road to Littlethorpe.

The first addition here was in 1871 when a timber platform shelter was erected on the Down platform. Plans show a shelter of the same size and in the same place to the present day, but it is unlikely to be the same one, although there is no record of a change. The current structure is a plain, pitched-roof shed in horizontal boarding.

In 1880 a single-storey, ladies waiting room (now a general waiting room) was added at the east side of the Station Master's house which allowed the existing one at the west end to be used for enlarging the booking office. At the same end a short section was removed to allow room for steps which still lead to the typical LNWR footbridge,

A postcard view of Narborough from the south.

120

Narborough, looking towards Hinckley, in 1968 very much as it is today but without the wooden waiting hut on the right. (Andrew Muckley)

Narborough in 1992.

provided in 1892. The bridge compliments the adjacent early type of LNWR signal box that protects the very busy level-crossing.

A year after the new bridge, a 24ft x 8ft 'portable' hut was erected at the opposite end of the station for use as a gentleman's waiting room. It was similar to the platform shelter, but in vertical boarding and removed in 1968. Platforms were lengthened in 1890 and again only 10 years later, but not raised to standard height until late in the 1950s.

Closure of the station came in March 1968 — but not for long. After a well-organised campaign (which started even before the station was closed) led by local headmaster Mr D. Williams, and with a large amount of financial backing from Blaby

RDC and the Parish Council, British Rail were persuaded to reopen the station. This was very significant as it was the first station in the country to be reopened after all the Beeching closures, and it set the trend for many more nationwide. Reopening was on 5 January 1970. The station has flourished since and the Councils' subsidies that were initially required have now been removed.

BLABY

The diminutive station was perched on an embankment just west of the bridge over Leicester Road, north of Blaby village. It originally consisted of one building, on the Down side, that was approached by an inclined footpath from the road. The modest building was rectangular, in narrow wooden boarding and with curved corrugated iron

121

An early picture of the Up-side general waiting room at Blaby before it was enlarged.

A view from Leicester Road, Blaby of the Down-side booking office which was destroyed by fire in 1914.

roof. Although quite small it contained booking office and separate waiting facilities. The platforms were completely of timber and incredibly short at only 57 yards. They were lengthened though, in 1887 and again only 16 years later.

In 1874 a general waiting room was approved for the Up side after years of passenger complaints, the style being another version of the LNWR's modular buildings in horizontal boarding with overhanging flat roof and decorated valance.

Events were then few until the station's main claim to fame came in the early hours of 12 July 1914 when the building on the Down platform was set ablaze. The Station Master was called from his house some distance away in Welford Road and with his policeman neighbour was able to rescue tickets and books, but even with the help of others, they could not save the building. The culprits were assumed to be Suffragettes as their literature was found scattered nearby and they were prone to this sort of activity at the time. Later, helpers at the fire were generously rewarded with ten shillings each from the railway company.

Although the burnt platform was soon replaced, five-and-a-half years were to elapse before a new building was erected. This was a modest structure, cheaply built of timber panelling, but it did have

Blaby in 1968 looking towards Leicester. (Andrew Muckley)

shapely wooden brackets supporting an inclined roof that extended over the platform to form a basic awning.

In contrast, the traditional style of the more distinguished building on the opposite platform was maintained when it was doubled in length at about the same time. This extension gave more waiting rooms and a second booking office, reached by a new inclined path from the road. A major part of the alterations, completed in 1920, included the raising of both timber platforms.

Despite the improvements, business declined to the point that a Station Master was not required from about 1930, the station then being controlled from Narborough. The station did last though, until closure of stopping services in 1968. Soon after, the station was again severely burnt, this time by young arsonists. Only the path that led to the Down side platform remains.

WIGSTON GLEN PARVA

This was not one of the line's original stations, but was opened during 1882 especially to serve an adjacent army barracks. Sole use by the soldiers did not last long, for a service for the general public was started on 1 April 1884. Opening as Glen Parva, it became Glen Parva for Wigston for a short time in 1887, but from then on was always called Wigston Glen Parva.

The platforms were situated in a cutting west of the Saffron Road overbridge with initially just one entrance, on the Up side of the bridge, where a hut was sited for the issue and collection of tickets.

Wigston Glen Parva in Edwardian times looking westwards. Buildings above the embankment belong to the army barracks.

The booking office at road level and station signal box at Wigston Glen Parva.

A 1950s view of Wigston Glen Parva looking towards the line's junction with the Midland Main Line.

From here an inclined path led down to the platform on which stood the station signal box at the bridge end.

For Glen Parva's station architecture we must thank the LNWR's Chief Mechanical Engineer, F.W.Webb, who designed the ubiquitous 'portable' hut. Constructed in timber, it was 8 feet wide and 8, 16 or 24 feet long. As well as the one mentioned at the entrance (the longest version) there was a similar type sited on the Up platform in 1887 for use as a waiting room, and in the same year the shortest version was sited at the station 'for the sole storage of biscuit boxes' (a large amount of biscuits were made in Wigston and despatched from all three of Wigston's stations).

A hut of 16 feet was also provided for the ladies on the Up platform in 1904 and another of similar length for use as a general waiting room erected on the Down platform in 1913. For this latter platform a flight of steps from road level had been provided in 1892. Despite all the plain huts the station was

never dull, winning best-kept station competitions on many occasions, helped by well-tended gardens.

In 1896 the Up platform was temporarily lengthened to allow ticket collection from the longest trains. This was brought about because facilities at the Leicester ticket platform were inadequate, especially for the large number of passengers attending the Royal Show at Leicester's Abbey Park that year. The extension was subsequently made permanent and used until Leicester became a 'closed' station (collecting its own tickets) in 1918.

There was no specially-built station house here, but Station Masters were accommodated nearby, usually in Blaby Road or Saffron Road. Between the wars trade declined such that a Station Master was not required and the station was administered from Leicester.

Closure came with the other stations in 1968, even though soldiers were still regular customers from the barracks next door. With its peculiar type of architecture, demolition of the station was soon effected with little more than the removal of the 'portable' huts.

SOUTH WIGSTON

Wigston is a large town once supporting three stations until their closure in the 1960s. However, with an upturn in rail travel late in the 1970s and precedents set with small stations springing up in other parts of the country, it was considered that one new station in Wigston could be viable. Local resident Dennis Taylor and his committee pursued the possibility for over six years, and finally, with the backing of a large grant from the County Council, they made it reality. It was a campaign by local residents which had similarities to the beginnings of other, much earlier stations in the County, Lilbourne, Croft, and Morcott for example.

With several dignitaries present and the band playing, the grand opening of South Wigston was performed on Saturday, 10 May 1986, and a special shuttle run to Leicester in order to publicise the main service which started the following Monday.

The station is situated in a wide cutting 300 yards east of where the Glen Parva station stood, and is approached by inclined paths from an established pedestrian bridge that spans the lines between Kirkdale Road and Kenilworth Road. Platforms are of concrete and staggered either side of the bridge, both with a bus-stop type shelter. A booking booth, manned at peak periods, was provided at the entrance to the Up platform, but lasted for only about four years — all passengers now paying on the train.

Since opening the station has been successfully supported and it seems appropriate that an area whose name derived from its first station (Wigston South — see Section 2) should again have a working station of its own. Flower gardens, seen at few stations nowadays, are an attractive feature.

South Wigston in 1997 from the Leicester platform.

The Down platform at South Wigston on the curve of the junction with the Midland Main Line.

125

ASHBY & NUNEATON JOINT RAILWAY (LNWR & MR)

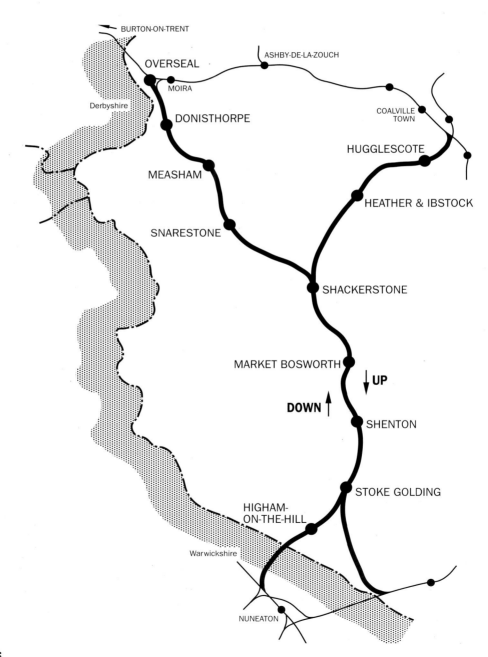

ASHBY & NUNEATON
JOINT RAILWAY (LNWR & MR)

This line ran from Nuneaton northwards to Moira Junction on the Leicester & Burton line, with a single line branch from Shackerstone to Coalville Junction, also on the Leicester & Burton line. Initially mineral trains (for which the railway was primarily built) were run, starting on 1 August 1873, whilst stopping goods trains commenced 18 days later and passenger trains on 1 September.

Although passenger traffic was of secondary importance this was not reflected in the 11 stations provided, all of which were quite generous affairs. They were from the Midland Railway's drawing board and all of the same basic, single-storey design, but with three variations in size (referred to by the Joint Committee as first, second and third class) and other detail differences. All had hipped roofs and shapely wooden brackets beneath the extended eaves.

The largest version was sited at the most important stations of Measham, Shackerstone and Market Bosworth, and consisted of a rectangular block with slightly protruding central section on the road side, in which was the entrance to the booking hall. The various waiting rooms could be reached through the hall and were situated either side of a waiting area, this area effectively a recess in the building at the platform side. It was separated from the platform by a large ornate screen, formed of iron pillars topped with decorative spandrels, and glazed between pillars above waist height — except for an opening at the centre. The screen's lower panels were of wood. To reduce maintenance costs the screen was removed in later years at all three stations with just the iron pillars retained.

Small double bays used as offices and conveniences were situated at both ends of the main block, and on all buildings, including the brick waiting shelter on the opposite platform, openings had sandstone surrounds and segmental heads with pronounced keystones. The waiting

An example of the first class style of station at Measham, taken from the south in the 1950s.
(M.H.Billington)

127

shelter also matched the main building with a hipped roof.

Passage between platforms at all the line's stations was by boarded crossing except at Shackerstone where a public footpath crossed the line and a bridge was provided.

There were versions of the second class design at Snarestone, Stoke Golding, Heather & Ibstock and Overseal. This design had the familiar Midland style twin pavilions joined by a short bay. The recess formed by the bay on the platform side was roofed and fronted by a glazed wooden screen. The screen was much shallower than at the larger stations and the glazing had a lozenge-pattern design.

Openings were very distinctive with large, round heads in white brick with contrasting blue brick quoins; at the front and rear of the pavilions the windows were paired. At one end only of each station, a flat-roofed outbuilding was attached.

At the remaining four stations, Donisthorpe, Hugglescote, Shenton and Higham-on-the-Hill, the design was similar to the version above but smaller. The screened recess on the platform side was the same, but because shallower pavilions were used, the linking bay protruded at the road side. Oddly, on just this protruding bay a decorated valance was attached. Windows were also different being the segmental-headed variety as seen on the first class buildings. Attached at one end was a small, hipped-roof convenience.

Platform shelters built with the two smaller designs were either of the brick style used at the first class stations or open-fronted timber ones with single sloping roof and valance. Like the main buildings these were of Midland design, as were the ample, two-storey station houses which were T-shaped in plan except at Market Bosworth which had an extra bay. (Similar standard station houses can be seen at the former Midland stations at Syston, Grimston and Old Dalby.) Inexplicably, at the three northernmost stations, Overseal,

A second class style at Snarestone, also showing the station house from the road side.

A third class example at Hugglescote taken in 1961 looking towards Shackerstone Junction. (H.W.Sadler)

Donisthorpe and Measham, a station house of the normal design was not provided and Station Masters had to manage with only ordinary terraced accommodation.

Arrangements for maintenance of the buildings, right up to LMS days in 1923, were for the LNWR to look after Shackerstone and all stations south, whilst the Midland maintained the remainder.

Passenger traffic would not have contributed much wear and tear to the buildings though, as it was never high. Passenger figures from the Midland Railway's records, reproduced in part in the Appendix, and recording bookings for only the Midland trains, indicate (with the reasonable assumption that the almost equal amounts of LNWR trains on the line were similarly loaded) that the passenger business was so meagre it could hardly have ever paid its way — especially at the three rural stations at the southern end of the line.

(The figures shown after the turn of the century are erratic due to a change in the pattern of the LNWR and Midland trains calling at the stations. This is marked at the two branch line stations, Hugglescote and Heather & Ibstock, where Midland trains en route to Coalville Town station ceased to call after 1916.)

Nevertheless, the LMS maintained services to all stations until 13 April 1931 after which, with the exception of Higham-on-the-Hill, they were manned only for the more profitable goods traffic.

Eventually, goods facilities were closed one by one, the last stopping goods trains running on the branch to Hugglescote in 1964 and the last on the main route was to Market Bosworth in 1968. Through freights ceased in 1971 and, at the northern end, Measham to Moira Junction was closed in stages between 1981 and 1985 as the local colliery trains were reduced.

During the declining years certain stations came to life very briefly during the summer months. This was for excursion traffic which lasted at some stations until 1962.

Happily there are still some services on the line. These are on a preserved section that runs south from Shackerstone — this station very much alive as the headquarters of the Shackerstone Railway Society. Their inaugural service was to Market Bosworth on 26 March 1978 and regular trains to Shenton started on 2 August 1992. With the terminous at Shenton adjacent to the site of the Battle of Bosworth the line is now known as the Battlefield Line:

OVERSEAL

This station had the rare distinction of being designed by the Midland but used only by the LNWR. It was open for just 17 years and used by the LNWR as a terminus station until they secured running powers over the Midland's line to Burton-on-Trent and Ashby. LNWR trains then only used the Midland's Moira station when running to Ashby, which allowed Overseal station to close for passengers from 1 July 1890.

A very old photograph of Overseal which closed in 1890. It was situated at the northern end of the line at the junction with the Leicester-Burton line seen in the foreground.

A postcard view of Donisthorpe looking north.

The station was situated only a few yards south of Moira West Junction, such that the end of the Up platform was adjacent to the main Leicester-Burton line and the platforms situated at the side of the sharp junction curve. The access drive was from the Overseal to Woodville road to the main building on the Down side. The platform shelter was of the brick variety.

The buildings were demolished in 1920, about three years after their closure for the goods business. During the goods-only days, control was by the Station Master at Moira.

The station was originally entitled Overseal & Moira, but company timetables showed it as just Overseal from March 1883.

DONISTHORPE

The station was reasonably close to the village and approached on the Down side of the line by a drive south of the road to Ashby. It was the only station not opened with the line, its building delayed until the growth of traffic at other stations could be assessed. The Joint Committee must have been reasonably confident about its potential though, as land for it had been purchased and a Station Master's house (in New Street) was in the course of construction when the line opened. The first train stopped on 1 May 1874.

The booking office was enlarged in 1901 and on the Up side a screen was added to the timber platform shelter in 1908. After closure for passengers, despite its continued use as a goods station until 1964, the buildings were soon removed — as early as 1936 — most probably because the buildings became unsafe due to mining subsidence which was prevalent in the area. A small, timber building was then used as a goods office.

In 1996 the cutting in which the station stood was infilled and landscaped. This has left no evidence of the station site.

MEASHAM

Here the line bridged the main A453 near the centre of the town with the station just to the south. A short drive, now Wilkes Avenue, led from the

Measham in the early part of the century looking towards Nuneaton.

Snarestone in Victorian times with south-bound freight train.

main road passing railway cottages (one of which was for the Station Master) to the large station forecourt which was on the Up side.

After closure in 1931 the station building was used by the goods yard staff and briefly in some years by passengers on summer excursions, the last in 1962.

Following railway use the station area became a car breaker's yard, the main building surviving, but not the waiting room on the opposite platform. Projected plans by Leicestershire County Council, who now own the building, are for the station's restoration and conversion into a museum and library.

SNARESTONE

Although always shown as Snarestone by the Midland, Snareston was used in the LNWR timetables where it remained without the 'e' until December 1900.

The short drive to the station, on the Up side, was from the junction of the Snarestone to Twycross and Appleby Magna roads and still leads to the station house. The house has recently been extended with a large extra bay on the former platform side. The station buildings, used for excursion trains until 1961, were removed, including the brick type of waiting shelter, in about 1970.

SHACKERSTONE

This station was eventually sited in the obvious place, at the junction with the Coalville branch, but only after many months of wrangling with the landowner, Earl Howe, who earnestly tried to have the station sited north of the junction so that it was convenient for his home at Gopsall Hall. He also tried to have the station called Gopsall, but to no avail, for it duly appeared in both company timetables as Shackerstone, although for a period between March 1883 and February 1900, the title Shackerstone Junction was used by the LNWR.

The station, now preserved, is sited at the end of a very long drive that leads from a lane east of Shackerstone village. The pleasant drive runs at the side of the Ashby canal to the Down side of the line and is still lined with trees provided by Earl Howe.

Shackerstone was the headquarters of the line Superintendent, but here he did not double as Station Master, unlike the situation at Melton Mowbray on the other joint line in the County, where, for the first few years, the same gentleman held both positions.

Special at this station is the footbridge that still links the north end of the platforms. It is necessary here as it carries a public footpath across the line. As far as can be ascertained it is the original bridge dating from 1881 and is of metal on polychrome-brick piers. On the Down side pier is now displayed the 'MR' terra cotta sign transferred from the demolished Coalville Town station, whilst on the Up side, one of the bridge's two flights of steps has been removed.

A well documented incident occurred when King Edward VII and Queen Alexandra arrived at the

Shackerstone in 1959. The line to Coalville branches northwards behind the signal box. (M.H.Billington)

Detail of the eaves and spandrels that once surmounted the glazed screens at Shackerstone.

A replica at Shackerstone of the brick type of waiting shelter used at most stations on the line.

station en route to Gopsall Hall and the door of the King's carriage could not be opened. Accounts often put the cause down to the height of the platform being increased especially for the visit, and that it had been raised too much. Actually, only a temporary wooden ramp had been provided to assist the King from his saloon and the problem was with the door jamming on the Royal train which was on its maiden journey.

The King had to use the door of the Queen's saloon from which the Queen had already alighted

— without a ramp. The incident, which the King took lightly, took place in front of a huge crowd at the heavily decorated station (which included temporary electric lighting) on 9 December 1902. (This date is often documented as 1906.)

At final closure the building was in poor condition despite being used as goods offices and for excursions (the last in 1962). By the time the Shackerstone Railway Society took over the premises for their headquarters in 1970 it was quite derelict. Excellent renovation work has now been carried out though, and as well as the provision of waiting and refreshment rooms, the building houses a superb museum — an Aladdin's cave of railway relics. The site entrance for visitors is along the old trackbed approached from the Shackerstone to Heather road.

Behind the station the station house is still in use and on the Up platform an excellent replica of the original brick shelter was completed in 1991 for use as a Society shop. Being in a conservation area the main building has now been given listing status.

HEATHER & IBSTOCK

Two roads run almost parallel from Heather to Ibstock and the station was sited between the roads midway between the two villages. There was a separate station approach from each road. Originally the title was Heather, but Ibstock,

growing rapidly, was added to the name in August 1894. Although on a single-line branch, there was a loop at the station and two platforms, the main building on the Down side and a wooden shelter opposite. The Midland style signal box was also on the Down platform.

After closure for passengers in April 1931, there were departures for a few years for local children's outings. Most of the buildings were demolished by the end of the 1940s, but the station house remains alongside the original approach road from the south.

HUGGLESCOTE

Like Heather & Ibstock there was a passing loop here and two platforms. They were in a cutting west of the road that runs southwards from the village to Bagworth, the main building being on the Down side. With the exception of the early

A south-bound LNWR 2-4-2T engine with just one carriage, from Loughborough Derby Road, waiting at Heather & Ibstock early this century.

Only the gentlemen's toilet block, platform shelter and signal box remain at Heather & Ibstock station in 1949. The goods shed is on the right.
(Stations U.K.)

*Hugglescote in 1957
looking towards
Shackerstone.
The station house can
be seen in the distance.
(Les Hales)*

*The rear of Hugglescote
in 1965, a year after the
goods yard closed.
(J. P. Alsop)*

years, a Midland signal box was positioned on the opposite platform, whilst next to the station building was a timber goods shed – unusual as all others on the line were brick.

The last summer excursions organised by the railway company were in the year of closure for regular use, 1931, and the main building survived until the early 1970s. Also on the site for a number of years was a redundant Midland signal box used as an office and store. Even the station house has now disappeared. Strangely, this was not sited near the road, but along a track, some 300 yards west of the station.

MARKET BOSWORTH

South of the road, one mile west of the village, a short drive still leads to the station and house on the Down side of the line. At one time a short flight of steps led from the road to the opposite platform descending a short embankment.

After the 1931 closure to passengers the station building was used for goods offices, and during the Second World War most of it was taken over by the army, who also enlarged the goods yard for use as a petrol distribution depot. Railway tankers were stored here and thousands of jerrycans filled for despatch by road for use in army vehicles. A network of narrow gauge lines was installed for use in the depot.

During their occupation the army built an undignified extension on the platform side of the main building for use as a cookhouse. This can still be seen, now part of the building which has been used by a motor engineer since shortly after the goods yard closed in 1968. The last excursion train to use the station was in 1962.

The opposite platform is used by the Shackerstone Railway Society and served as their terminus until the extension to Shenton was

A photocall at Market Bosworth in 1883, only ten years after the line opened. The engine is a Midland 2-2-2 No.35 facing north.

Ivy-clad Market Bosworth in 1905.

Market Bosworth in 1962 (B. J. Smith)

opened. Unfortunately, the brick waiting shelter on this platform was demolished before the Society was formed and so a timber shelter (designed in LNWR style with large flat canopy) was erected in 1987 to serve as a booking office. An additional timber building, again in LNWR style but with hipped roof, was transferred from Chester Road station (Birmingham) and rebuilt on the platform in the early 1990s.

SHENTON

This station was in a very rural area and as a result has the distinction of having the lowest amount of passenger traffic of all the County's Midland-associated stations that were open for any reasonable time. Bookings for Midland trains averaged less than 10 per week for several years

and was probably used less than stations of other companies including the small halts on the Charnwood Forest Line (Section 10). The station was situated at the side of the Dadlington road midway between two small villages, Shenton and Sutton Cheney.

Although classified as only a third class station, an extra rectangular bay was provided that stood alone just north of the main block on the Down platform. It matched the style of the main building, but the reason for the extra accommodation cannot be found. By the early 1950s, along with the platforms, this block was the only part of the station still standing and it eventually found use as a souvenir shop for visitors to the Bosworth Battlefield centre nearby.

An early view of the station site at Shenton looking north.

This separate part of the main station building at Shenton still stands. (M.H.Billington)

The booking office building from Humberstone Road Leicester being rebuilt on the Up side at Shenton in June 1993. Bosworth battlefield is behind this building.

Trains again used the station when the privately-run line was extended from Shackerstone. The first train was on 2 August 1992 and for the new service the Up platform was rebuilt to standard height. The inaugural day saw the first stopping passenger train since the station's closure in 1931 as, understandably, no excursions departed from here.

The platform shelter had been the brick version, but now on the same Up platform stands a re-erected station building that has been meticulously moved brick by brick from Humberstone Road, Leicester (Section 2). It is a building of the correct period for the line and its Midland style is in keeping with the line's general design of stations. The relocated building was erected in 1993 and is used as a waiting room, shop and for exhibitions.

Although listing maintained its survival at Humberstone Road, the building has now been de-listed. Shenton's station house remains occupied by the main road.

STOKE GOLDING

Although all three of the largest variety of station on the line remain, Stoke Golding is the only one of the two smaller varieties that survives. It is situated ½ mile west of Stoke Golding village on the north side of the road and has now been converted for residential use — fortunately without significant modification to its original design.

The station house also remains, with modern extensions, at the entrance of the short station drive, but the brick waiting shelter on the Down

The only surviving building of the smaller stations is at Stoke Golding seen here in 1962. (Les Hales)

The view north at Stoke Golding.
(M.H.Billington)

platform has been removed. A tastefully renovated building on the site is the goods shed, now used as a modern factory unit.

The station's last use was for an excursion in 1962.

HIGHAM-ON-THE-HILL

The original plans did not include a station here, the intention being for Higham residents to use the station at Stoke Golding. Letters from Higham villagers to the Joint Committee protesting about this were heeded though, and a station was opened with the line, although without goods facilities. A special drive was constructed (now Station Drive) running northwards from the main road over an existing footpath on the west side of the village. This led to the platforms, set in a cutting on the east side of the drive, and was continued to bridge the line in place of the footpath.

Unlike all of the line's other stations the main building was not on a platform but situated near the drive at the top of the railway embankment. A sloping path led from the building to the Up platform. A platform shelter was on the Down platform and the station house, the only surviving part of the site, was next to the main building.

The company's original decision not to provide facilities here was surely the correct one as the station hardly ever paid its way and it is surprising that it lasted until 1931. In the last three years that figures are available (1920-2) the average receipts from passengers and parcels on Midland trains amounted to only £84 per year, whilst the Midland's annual expenditure at the station was £924.

Because there were no goods facilities, the station buildings were not required after closure and were soon demolished. The platforms were removed later in 1936.

A typical Midland Railway design incorporating polychrome brickwork was used for most of the station houses on the line. This one is at Higham-on-the-Hill in 1991. (There is no known photograph of the station building which stood behind the house.)

CHARNWOOD FOREST RAILWAY

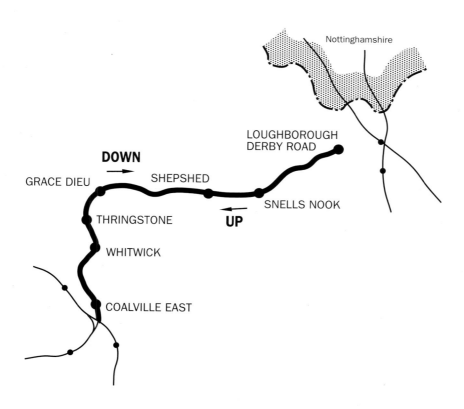

CHARNWOOD FOREST RAILWAY

This single line was built as a continuation of the Shackerstone to Coalville branch of the Ashby & Nuneaton Railway and ran from Coalville through to a terminus at Loughborough. It opened for all traffic on 16 April 1883 although specials had run before this: on 29 January two train loads of trucks had taken passengers along the line to a concert in Loughborough in aid of a worker disabled whilst employed on the line, and on 1 March a special trip solely for the press had been run from Loughborough to Coalville.

Although built and owned by the independent Charnwood Forest Railway Company, the LNWR invested heavily in the line during its planning stage and ran the line from its opening right through to the 1923 grouping. Its four original stations at Coalville East, Whitwick, Shepshed and Loughborough Derby Road were the responsibility of the owning company and the LNWR had no part in their design.

Unfortunately financial success was not part of the line's history, and company minutes are mainly concerned with the survival of the business rather than its development. There is reference, however, to two main initiatives designed to improve profitability. Firstly, was the introduction of cheap-to-run rail motor services, which started on 18 June 1906 between Loughborough and Shackerstone (occasionally as far as Market Bosworth) and secondly, for use with the new vehicles, three halts were opened on 2 April the following year.

The halts, at Thringstone, Grace Dieu and Snells Nook, were instigated by the LNWR in a desperate attempt to attract passengers and were similar to many other wayside halts springing up at this time throughout the country in the hope of competing with new omnibus services.

The halts on this line were merely platforms 6 feet wide, 33 inches high and just 60 feet long and made up of old sleepers. Waiting huts were added later. At first passengers boarding at the halts paid on the train, but when the huts were provided the guard issued the tickets – less efficiently it would appear – from the huts. It was also the guard's duty to tend the oil lamps at the platforms.

Despite the attempts to increase passenger traffic, it remained meagre and halts and stations lasted for regular use only until 13 April 1931, although the stations did continue in use as goods offices. The last passenger traffic of all, except for enthusiasts' specials, was in 1939 when the four stations saw their last holiday excursions. Immediately after the war an attempt was made by the Coalville Trades Council to gain support for reopening the line, but it was realised that passengers had become too used to the more convenient bus services, especially as all the stations, except Whitwick, were well away from their town centres.

With two other stations serving Loughborough for goods, the traffic at the Derby Road station was low and this was the first on the line to close completely — from 31 October 1955. The goods facilities at the line's remaining stations finished during 1963 with the final train running from the granite quarry at Shepshed on 11 December that year:

COALVILLE EAST

This station was not at all prominent in the town, being tucked away at the end of Charnwood Street off the main London Road.

Contrary to most railway company standards of the time, the Station Master's house was not built separately, but as part of the station — cheapness being very important on this line. The building comprised a two-storey block, the first floor and part of the ground floor for the Station Master, whilst the remainder of the ground floor and a single-storey bay, which ran to the south, was for

Coalville East in 1951 – facing north. The spur on the right served the Whitwick Granite Company sidings. (National Railway Museum)

Coalville East, about 1953. (M.H.Billington)

the usual offices and waiting rooms. To alleviate the building's modest design a band of dentil decoration ran round the middle of the whole block, and a porchway, with open arches on its three sides, protruded from the single-storey section over the booking office entrance.

Roofs were hipped including that over the porchway and plain, square-headed windows were used. On the platform side a flat canopy, on rather slender pillars, ran the length of the two-storey section, but was removed around the time of the last War.

The line was single through the station requiring only one platform, on which stood the square station signal box at the northern end. Station name changes were frequent; opening as Coalville East, this became Coalville from May 1905 and

Coalville (LNW) from May 1910. In June 1924 Coalville East was again used. The station was removed in 1970 to make way for a new housing development.

WHITWICK

The line passed conveniently through the centre of the village and crossed beneath the main road (North Street) in a fairly deep cutting. The station was sited by the north side of the bridge where the main building can still be seen. To gain room for building the station and its small forecourt, cottages had first to be removed.

The main part of the building is effectively two-storey, standing at the south end of the single, Down-side platform with the top storey at road level. Originally the upper floor contained the booking hall and booking office, with other rooms

A pre-1909 view of Whitwick's single platform looking north.

Whitwick in 1965.
(R.M.Casserley)

The former road-level booking office at Whitwick in 1983.

A sketch of Thringstone from the south-east based on site plans.

below. The waiting rooms were in a separate building on the platform, and reached by a wide flight of steps from the booking hall.

Roofs on both buildings were hipped and openings square and plain, although on the platform side of the general waiting room there were two wide arches, originally open, but enclosed with glazed screens in 1909. Dentil decoration surrounds the main building.

By 1901 it had become apparent that the station was unnecessarily large and so the booking hall was converted for letting as a shop; presumably tickets were then issued from one of the platform buildings. First use of the shop was by a barber, followed by a tailor in the 1920s and 30s. It was then a hairdressers again (complete with red and white pole) for many years until replaced by an ironmonger. Lastly, after the local council had bought the property and renovated it in 1986, it became the home of the Whitwick Historical Group.

Towards the end of the 1960s the derelict waiting rooms on the platform were removed and the wide stairway replaced by basic metal steps from the station forecourt. Perhaps because of its cramped position a house was not provided with the station, but instead, accommodation was rented for the Station Master in the village — for a long time in Church Lane. Unfortunately, the station is not yet the listed building it deserves to be.

THRINGSTONE

Only ¾ mile from Whitwick was Thringstone halt, situated in a cutting south of Grace Dieu Road that runs eastward from the village. The short platform was on the village side of the line and reached by steps from the road overbridge.

A hut was provided at the back of the platform in 1914 — seven years after the halt had opened — and only then after several requests from residents. It was a standard LNWR 'portable' type, 16ft x 8ft, of timber construction and with a plain pitched roof. It was 'charged to the Charnwood Company'.

After closure in 1931 the hut was let for a short time to the local cobbler, but it is doubtful if this boosted the income of the LMS a great deal despite their providing a brake van stove into the rental! The embankment where the halt stood has now been lowered to form the garden of a bungalow.

GRACE DIEU

Before the line was opened and again in 1897 the local council requested a station at Grace Dieu, but both attempts were unsuccessful. It is probable that the idea was for residents of Osgathorpe, Belton and possibly Thringstone to be served rather than Grace Dieu itself where there was only a large manor house.

As it happened, 10 years after the last request a halt was provided and most of the traffic, in the summer at least, was from tourists visiting the ruined Priory (after which the halt was named) and the delightful surrounding countryside. A few factory workers from the villages to the north were, however, regular customers.

The halt was located just west of where the line bridged over the main Ashby to Loughborough road, with the single platform on the south side. It was reached by a path and steep flight of steps from the road to the top of the embankment, where a waiting hut, similar to that at Thringstone, was sited from early 1911. The embankment has now mostly been removed, but parts can still be discerned.

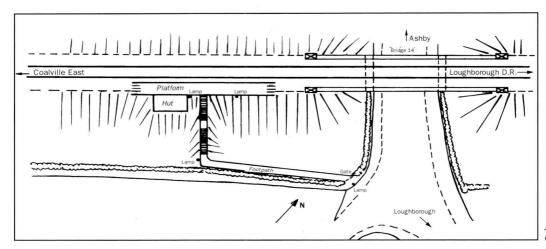

*A plan of
Grace Dieu*

SHEPSHED

Shepshed station (originally named Sheepshed until May 1888) was reached from the end of Spring Lane at the southern end of the town. There was also access from the west, to either side of the line, using drives that started from Charnwood Road. Like Coalville East, the station building was on the Down side, and it appears that the buildings were identical, including awning and protruding porch with arched openings at the entrance.

At this station though, there was a passing loop served by a second platform. On the Up side a basic, open waiting shelter with single inclined roof was sited and on the Down side, just east of the main building, was the small station signal box.

Outstanding aspects in the early years were the prolific, prize-winning flower gardens that even included rustic trellis work. The beds opposite the main building were particularly large and once featured the word 'Shepshed' in large ornate lettering of white stones.

After closure to passengers in 1931 the house remained occupied and some of the offices used for goods business. On complete closure in 1963 the property was bought by the local council, the single-storey section removed, and for a short time the house occupied by a council worker. After a period of dereliction the building was then demolished in 1974 and a new approach road, Old Station Close, built on the trackbed. This now gives access to an industrial estate that covers the site.

*The north elevation of
Shepshed taken in 1960.
(Les Hales)*

Two platforms were provided at Shepshed, seen here facing Coalville in about 1910.

SNELLS NOOK

This was situated where the line crossed over a drive leading into the grounds of the former Garendon Hall. The drive starts at a lodge almost opposite Snells Nook Lane on the Ashby Road from Loughborough.

The platform and waiting hut were west of the bridge over the drive and reached by a short flight of steps ascending the embankment. The hut dated from 1911 and was standard LNWR, although larger than at the other two halts, probably a 24ft x 8ft version.

Users of the halt included guests of the Hall's owner, Squire de Lisle (who had originally helped promote the halt) and also trippers to the deer park within the Hall grounds. Particularly busy times were when the Leicestershire Yeomanry and the Territorials held their training camps at Garendon before the First World War. The halt was so well used on these occasions, receiving crowds of visitors, that the LNWR had to provide temporary platform accommodation. (The press reported in 1911 that during two weeks of camps, over 17,000 passengers were moved through the halt. Similarly, Whitwick station was particularly busy when military training camps were held at nearby High Tor.) The halt was also popular with golfers travelling to the Longcliffe Golf Club.

At the site the embankment remains, but the adjacent bridge has been removed.

LOUGHBOROUGH DERBY ROAD

This terminal station stood west of the main A6 (Derby Road) 1/2 mile north of the town centre on a site now occupied by a petrol station. This was not the originally intended site though, for in the 1876 act for building the line the designated site was adjoining the Midland station across the town in Nottingham Road. It would have been convenient for transferring passengers, but probably the high costs enforced revision of the plans.

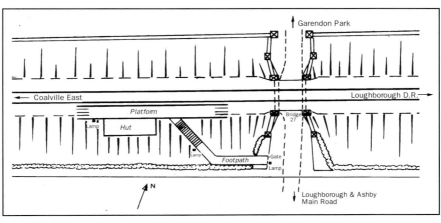

A plan of Snells Nook

Although the most important station on the line, it was not the most imposing building. Single-storey and very plain, it was quite inferior to Coalville East and Shepshed, both of which had an integral, two-storey Station Master's house to create some sort of dignity (Loughborough's Station Master had to rely on locally-rented accommodation.) The poor design was again probably due to lack of finance more than anything else.

The station comprised two adjoining blocks at right-angles, the larger one running behind the buffer stops and facing Derby Road. This contained the main offices, including centrally-placed booking hall, at the entrance to which was a projecting porch with arched openings similar to those at Coalville and Shepshed. The other block, to the north, ran parallel to a single platform and contained passenger facilities and a side exit. Although there were four lines running into the station only one was used for the few passenger trains, the remainder mainly employed for wagon storage as the goods yard was adjacent.

Covering both the platform and concourse behind the buffers were flat canopies supported by slender, iron pillars topped with decorative spandrels. Roofs were mainly hipped, and similar to the line's other buildings, chimneys were tall and windows square-headed, but here there was no dentil decoration.

Two minor amenities the station could boast were a W. H. Smith bookstall, open for a few years in the last century, and the provision, in 1890, of a boiler for filling footwarmer cans (the predecessor to train heating). Little else is recorded before the closure to passengers in 1931.

The station then continued for goods only, with the buildings used mostly for storage, until complete closure in 1955. A builder's merchant then used part of the site and on at least one occasion part of the building was utilised as a polling station. Demolition occurred at the end of 1965 with no great loss to the town's architecture.

The end of the line at Loughborough Derby Road in the 1930s.

Loughborough Derby Road, in 1962. (Neil Cossons)

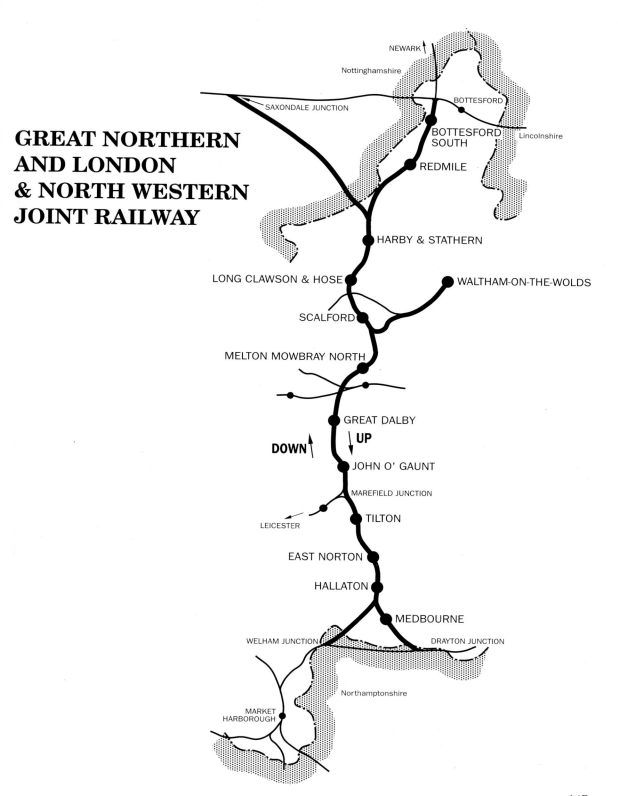

GREAT NORTHERN AND LONDON & NORTH WESTERN JOINT RAILWAY

NEWARK

Nottinghamshire

SAXONDALE JUNCTION

BOTTESFORD

BOTTESFORD SOUTH

Lincolnshire

REDMILE

HARBY & STATHERN

LONG CLAWSON & HOSE

WALTHAM-ON-THE-WOLDS

SCALFORD

MELTON MOWBRAY NORTH

GREAT DALBY

DOWN ↑

UP ↓

JOHN O' GAUNT

MAREFIELD JUNCTION

LEICESTER

TILTON

EAST NORTON

HALLATON

MEDBOURNE

WELHAM JUNCTION

DRAYTON JUNCTION

Northamptonshire

MARKET HARBOROUGH

GREAT NORTHERN AND LONDON & NORTH WESTERN JOINT RAILWAY

With the exception of a spur at the northern end from Stathern to Saxondale Junction, practically the whole of the line ran within Leicestershire, running north to south from Bottesford Junction to the Welham and Drayton Junctions on the Rugby & Stamford line.

Services started in stages, all in 1879. North of Melton, including the spur, goods traffic commenced on 30 June; this was extended to Twyford on 13 October, and to the remaining southern section on 1 November. For passengers a service started from Nottingham to Melton via Saxondale Junction on 1 September, but the main north to south route did not begin until 15 December. The short spur from Hallaton to Drayton Junction was only opened for passengers when a service started from the Leicester branch (Section 12) to Peterborough on 2 July 1883.

The stations provided for the relatively few passengers in this sparsely populated area were pleasant and substantial. Except for the two important stations at Melton Mowbray and Redmile they were all very similar, single-storey structures, despite the two owning companies having separate responsibility for design (as well as the line's engineering). Stations from Tilton northwards were by the Great Northern and those on the southern section by the LNWR. (The LNWR were also responsible for the stations and engineering on the spur outside the county between Stathern and Saxondale Junction.) Division of responsibility was different for maintenance and administration, with the LNWR taking charge of Melton and stations to the south, and the GNR the remainder.

For their part the GNR sub-contracted the engineering and architecture, employing the well-established company, J.Frasers of Leeds. Their Melton and Redmile station designs were quite special and described separately, but the remainder were virtually identical, rectangular blocks with an unusual half-hipped (gambrel) roof. Attached at both ends were flat-roofed bays containing conveniences and offices, each end wall decorated with ball finials. The best aspect of all was the elaborate cast-iron bracketry which supported a cantilevered flat awning that ran the length of the main block. The brackets were very decorative with a large sun motif at their heel.

Waiting amenities on the opposite platform were very generous, the building being virtually identical to that on the main side except shorter, having no booking facilities. At Harby & Stathern the minor building differed, having a second canopy at the rear as it stood on an island platform.

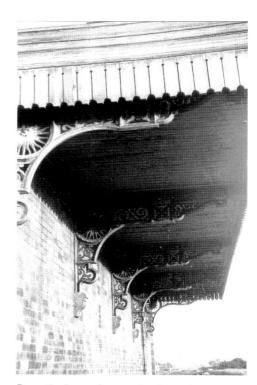

Decorative ironwork supporting the awning at Harby & Stathern.
(B.J.Smith)

Noticeable at each GNR station were the square lamp rooms, built separately from the main building, and with a distinctive pointed roof. The large, two-storey Station Masters' houses were also, in the main, common with an exception at Long Clawson & Hose where a company cottage had to suffice.

Almost identical to the GNR stations were the three designed by the LNWR at East Norton, Hallaton and Medbourne. Because of their similarity it was obvious that there was collaboration in the design between the two companies, probably because the Joint Committee insisted that both approved each other's plans. Perhaps another reason was that the LNWR could not use their modest, standard type of timber structure, normally used for their minor stations at this time, as there would have been a distinct imbalance of standards. The practical solution would have been

an identical design, but as it happened there were just detail differences.

The LNWR used less ornate brackets, the main roofs were plain hipped and there were no ball finials. Instead, decorative bands of light brickwork were employed at eave level and blue bricks used to dress the square-headed openings. There was actually more difference in the station houses – the LNWR ones being larger and much more elaborately styled than their Great Northern partners.

During planning of the line consideration was given for stops at Thorpe Satchville and Launde Wood (for the Abbey and Loddington) but neither came to fruition, Burrow & Twyford (later called John O'Gaunt) and East Norton respectively taking priority.

The plain style of Great Northern station house and cottages at Great Dalby in 1985 .

Contrasting style of the LNWR-designed station house at East Norton taken the same year.

Company minutes reveal little happening to the stations over the years, illustrated by the fact that one of the most interesting orders was 'that all waiting room walls are to be distempered french grey instead of papered'! With no major alterations stations must have been ample for their needs, although in 1888 standard LNWR huts were erected at most of the stations for the storage of small goods hitherto kept in the booking office or waiting rooms.

In the same year individual passenger bookings and receipts appeared in Joint Committee minutes — figures not often found in the records of either company. They were for three months, July-September 1888, and show briefly how the revenue of the stations compared in their early days:

Redmile	Bookings	3,175	Receipts	£223
Harby & Stathern	,,	6,081	,,	£471
Long Clawson & Hose	,,	2,295	,,	£104
Scalford	,,	2,507	,,	£147
Melton Mowbray	,,	11,184	,,	£1,222
Great Dalby	,,	1,833	,,	£86
John O'Gaunt	,,	4,770	,,	£371
Tilton	,,	1,416	,,	£176
East Norton	,,	2,915	,,	£277
Hallaton	,,	2,961	,,	£272
Medbourne	,,	999	,,	£65

The least used of the above stations at that time, Medbourne, was the first to close when traffic on the Hallaton to Drayton Junction curve was stopped from 1 April 1916 as a war economy measure.

Later, fortunes of all the stations were to suffer. From more detailed statistics available for some of the stations during the post-grouping era (listed in the Appendix) a rapid decline can be seen from the LNER part of the records, which can be assumed to be typical of all stations on the line for both companies. This led to the next closures following the Second War.

These started with the Harby to Bottesford section when the direct Leicester-Grantham services were finished from 10 September 1951. On the rest of the line regular passenger trains ceased from 7 December 1953, although an un-timetabled train for workmen continued to run between Market Harborough and East Norton ending from 20 May 1957. A similar service (but in the timetable) ran

along the Leicester line (Section 12) to John O'Gaunt and finished from 29 April the same year. Also originating from that line was the East Coast excursion traffic via Melton Mowbray, the last running on 9 September 1962.

Freight working ceased in sections: East Norton southwards from 4 November 1963, Marefield Junction to Melton from 1 June 1964, to Melton from the north from 7 September 1964, and rail connections to the Stathern Ironstone quarries and Redmile Petrol Depot severed in the early 1970s.

Of the passenger buildings, sadly none have survived of either company, most being removed only a few years after closure. All of the station houses survive, however, except at Melton, and in most cases sets of employees cottages can be seen at the station sites.

Included at the end of this section is the station at Waltham-on-the-Wolds (often printed as just 'Wold') built by the GNR at the end of a single-line branch that ran eastward from a point south of Scalford station. The four-mile branch was primarily for ironstone traffic, for which it opened in 1881, but the official opening of Waltham was as a goods station on 2 April 1883.

The station was built in the hope of running a regular passenger service, but this was never initiated and the station's only use for passengers was for specials, the first in 1882. Each time passenger trains were run permission was needed from the Board of Trade as the line was never passed for passenger use. This also applied for a few hunting specials and the occasional military train that served training camps on the branch:

BOTTESFORD SOUTH

During the line's planning the first intention was for high and low level exchange stations at Bottesford where the Joint Line's continuation to Newark (by the Great Northern) crossed beneath the existing Nottingham to Grantham line. However, the idea was abandoned with the building of the spur from Stathern to Saxondale Junction, allowing Harby & Stathern station to be used as a transfer point. So for this line a separate station was provided in Bottesford just west of the village, south of the old main road to Nottingham.

It was known initially as Bottesford New but was soon changed to Bottesford South from May

Much-modernised station cottages at Bottesford South in 1991.

1880. It was not even this for long, however, as 'expenditure was considerably greater than receipts' and the station closed from 1 May 1882.

For what purpose the buildings were then used is unknown. They were not utilised for goods processing as the goods siding, south of the station, was quickly removed and this business was carried out at the other Bottesford station on the Nottingham to Grantham line. Whatever their use, they survived a long time into the inter-War years.

The station house, on the east approach road to the station, was occupied by the signal man on the station's early closure and the building can still be seen, now much extended and modernised. On the opposite side of the station site company cottages also remain.

REDMILE

The main road through Redmile runs in one direction north-westerly to where the station stood on the south side of the road, and in the opposite direction directly to Belvoir Castle 2½ miles from the station. This is significant as the close proximity of the castle, home of the Duke of Rutland, had a great bearing on the station's design. Use by the Duke was expected and as he owned much of the land through which the Joint Line ran, it was reasonable that the station had special treatment — indeed he was sent the station plans for his approval before the building commenced.

Ducal influence made the station at Redmile very special - seen here in 1949, viewed from the north.
(Stations U.K.)

Elaborate treatment at the entrance to the Duke of Rutland's waiting room at the north-eastern end of Redmile station.

The most outstanding difference from the line's other small stations was the provision of an extra waiting room at the northern end of the main building specifically for the Duke and his guests. Over its entrance was a 'porte cochere' in elaborately carved oak with hipped, glazed roof and either side were squat square towers, one complete with pole for the Duke's standard. Inside, the waiting room was lavishly panelled in oak and the same wood used along with marble for a magnificent fireplace surround, the centrepiece of which was a carved illustration of 'the chase' in sight of Belvoir Castle.

Running the length of the building on the platform side was a glazed ridge and furrow awning – the end of each ridge gabled. It was supported on iron columns and at either end were patterned, glazed screens. Almost centrally a bay window projected onto the platform. There was also a profusion of carved-brick decoration on the building. The most noticeable was in swag form on the two entrance towers and on the building's gable ends — that on the north side depicting the Duke's coat of arms.

On the other platform there was little special about the building. It was similar to others on the line except slightly larger, with hipped roof and more decorated valance. For the Duke to transfer easily to this side of the line, special steps were let into the platform walls leading to a boarded crossing. They were covered during normal station use but rarely employed.

On opening, the station was designated Red Mile & Belvoir, but was soon shown in company timetables as Redmile for Belvoir — though not officially until 1886. This name remained until 1924 when just Redmile was used.

At the time of the Second World War a rail-served petrol depot was installed south of the station site and attended by troops who had free access to the station. Unfortunately they wrecked much of the building and in 1950 major renovation was required. This included complete removal of the grand 'porte cochere' and also removal of the glass awning except for two bays over the middle of the platform.

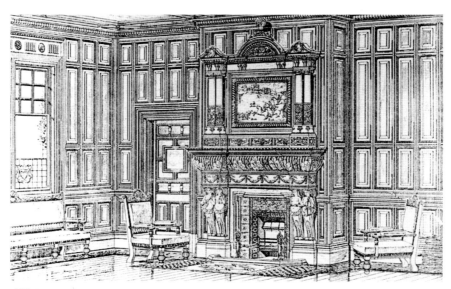

The interior design for the private waiting room at Redmile.

Early in 1951 the station was effectively closed for two months. Trains were regularly cancelled in the early 1950s due to shortage of coal and the only ones which stopped at Redmile were amongst those regularly cancelled. When normal services were resumed in March understandably passengers were few and the station remained open only until 10 September that year when the Leicester-Grantham trains ceased.

The buildings were removed in about 1954, the oak panelling from the Duke's waiting room being carefully removed for reuse, but where is unknown. Still to be seen on the station drive are the station house and cottages in virtually original condition, the house displaying some decorative brickwork that distinguishes it, like the station, from the more common types on the line.

HARBY & STATHERN

The line bridged the road midway between the villages of Harby and Stathern, a convenient place it would seem for the station, but at this point only the station house and cottages were built. The station itself was positioned at the end of a very long drive running southwards from the road for about $\frac{1}{3}$ mile and must have seemed very inconvenient to passengers. The reason for the long approach was that as this was an exchange station (passengers changing here between the Newark line trains and trains from the Nottingham to Grantham line) a large area was required which would have been expensive to build on the high embankment needed near the road.

The station layout included a wide island platform, west of the Down main line, and to the north of this a turntable — necessary when trains terminated here in the line's early years. There was also a bay at the south end of the opposite platform, formed a few years after opening by extending the goods-dock line behind the platform. The main building on this side was conventional, but the other, being on an island platform, had doorways repeated at front and rear and had two canopies.

Looking south at Harby & Stathern. Most of the building on the left (with bay platform behind) was burnt down in 1946.

The island exchange platform at Harby & Stathern, 1953. (H.C.Casserley)

The intention when building the line was for the station to be called Stathern, but only a week before opening it was changed to Harby & Stathern to avoid possible confusion with Hathern. In the early days the station must have been reasonably busy as a request was made for a separate refreshment room, but this was declined.

Little of note happened at the station until the early hours of 27 December 1946 when a fire tore through the main building, apparently started by gypsy youths who had been rifling the safe. The station's remoteness made it a prime target. The building was gutted and only the porter's room, at the south end, could be used again, although it needed a new pitched roof.

The station was little used at this time and rebuilding not thought worthwhile — not even temporary buildings were required. Instead, just the building on the island platform was used with most of the general waiting room converted into a booking office. This was found quite suitable, although somewhat inconvenient to passengers for the remaining seven years that the station was open.

The station house, cottages, goods shed and lamp room remain, but nothing is left of the station, where a coal merchant occupies the site.

LONG CLAWSON & HOSE

Two miles to the south of Hose village a drive from the main road led to the Down side of the station that was just north of Hose tunnel. Long Clawson was also two miles away, but by no means direct. In 1887, therefore, its villagers requested that the Joint Committee build a new, direct road to the station, so halving the distance — but this was rejected.

The station actually opened as Long Clawson, but after various requests from Hose villagers, including the clergy, it was changed to Long Clawson & Hose in October 1884. The vicar of Hose also made an unusual request in 1893 asking if he could conduct Sunday services in the station waiting room. This was declined but, had it not, this would have been an extraordinary double use of a working station typical of situations in the remoter parts of Scotland.

Unusual was that this was the only station on the Joint Line without a house of standard design for the Station Master; instead he was given one of the company cottages that still stand near the road. The station buildings were quickly removed after the 1953 closure and the site is now completely overgrown.

SCALFORD

This was on the north side of the road, just ½ mile west of Scalford village with the main building on the Up side. Running almost up to the southern end of the building was a bay platform, similar to Harby & Stathern, but here it contained two roads and only one platform face. The bay was intended for a regular shuttle service to Waltham-on-the-Wolds, but as this was never introduced, its only use for passengers was for annual shuttles to the Waltham fair and Croxton racecourse.

Long Clawson & Hose in 1953. The train from which the picture was taken is travelling south, about to enter Hose tunnel. (W.F.Deebank)

An 8F at Scalford running round its train bound for Waltham-on-the-Wolds in 1959.
(J.Spencer Gilks)

The main building at Scalford viewed from the Down platform.

Different from other stations on the line was the siting of the signal box. Here it was on the platform next to the standard type of waiting block on the Down side.

Closure came with the other stations in 1953 and since the station's removal a house with extensive gardens has been built on the site. The Station Master's house and cottages remain, but the former is almost beyond recognition as a standard railway building after much alteration.

MELTON MOWBRAY NORTH

The station was reasonably well situated on the north side of the town on the east side of Scalford Road. From the road a short drive curved off to the front of the main building. As this was the most important station on the line the Joint Committee went to great lengths to create some sort of showpiece, although not really justified by the small amount of traffic generated. Competition with the town's Midland station was probably the main reason for elaboration in its design.

The structure was not grand, only single-storey, the aim being to impress by the lavish decoration rather than size. This entailed extensive use of carved brickwork and terra-cotta mouldings, examples on the outside of the station being on the gable ends and within the three cross-gables which punctuated the very long frontage. The most impressive work included the coat of arms of the GNR and the LNWR's Britannia but, oddly, this was at the eastern end of the building away from the main public approach. On the platform

The approach road to
Melton Mowbray
North photographed
during the inter-war
years.

A lengthy job cleaning
the glass at Melton
Mowbray North,
although most of the
glass was removed soon
after this was taken in
the late 1940s.
(Stations U. K.)

A south-bound train
about to run into
Melton Mowbray
North on the last day
of regular passenger
traffic in 1953.
(D.E.Shepherd)

156

side there was also a profusion of terra-cotta above all main entrances, whilst other openings were surmounted with brick hoods.

Also impressive were the iron and glass ridged canopies covering each platform, the supporting cast-iron columns being far from plain and arranged down the centre of very wide platforms. The canopy ridges were gable-ended, topped with small ball finials, and on their lower edge ran an unusual cast-iron valance. The canopies were similar to those at Redmile as were the glazed screens at the canopy ends.

In the main building were all the usual offices and in addition were, at one time, waiting rooms for both classes, refreshment rooms (including dining room, regularly used by town folk) bookstall and, until 1912, the offices of the Joint Line Superintendent. This last position was jointly held by the Station Master for the first two years.

A large, square skylight and tall chimneys were dominant on each of the platform buildings, the buildings connected by a wide subway that passed beneath the tracks. The subway was lined with white, glazed bricks. Also below ground level, rather unusually, were the kitchens and living quarters for the caterers. Accommodation for the Station Master and cottages for other employees, were provided beyond a pleasant grass and wooded area to the front of the main building.

Platform detail, including subway entrance, in 1953. 'North' was not part of the station nomenclature when the 'Hawkseye' style of sign was provided. (D.E.Shepherd)

A WD Austerity heading a freight train northwards through Melton Mowbray in 1961. (M.A.Cooke)

*The minor platform building
at Great Dalby, 1953.
(D.E. Shepherd)*

*Great Dalby in 1956 with an approaching
excursion train from the East Coast .
(W. F. Deebank)*

Strangely, there was no official suffix to the station name to distinguish it from the other Melton station until 1958 when 'North' was added. (North had been used for the goods station since 1950.) Until then confusion must have been very common, although in Bradshaw's Railway Guide and local timetables, suffixes such as 'Joint Stn', 'GN' or 'LNE' were sometimes added.

Maintenance costs of such a large station must have been high compared with the low passenger usage. No doubt this led to removal of the canopy glazing (except for small areas above the centre of the platform) and also the end screens by about 1950. After closure of the local services in 1953 deterioration of the building set in and the station's only use then was for the summer services

to Skegness and Mablethorpe. The last was on 9 September 1962 and by that time the buildings were badly neglected and the platforms covered by a mass of wild vegetation.

During the next few years the main building was used as additional premises for a local dairy-farming company before demolition came, along with the station housing, in 1970. The whole site is now covered with industrial buildings, but one very small portion has survived; the depiction in brick of the Joint Companies' arms is now displayed at the Snibston Discovery Park at Coalville.

GREAT DALBY

There was nothing particularly special about this station, being one of the standard GNR-designed structures on a conventional layout. It was ¹/₂ mile west of the village, north of the road to Ashby Folville, a short drive leading to the main building on the Up side.

Although it saw a reasonable number of passengers, revenue was not high as most booked journeys were for the short trip into Melton (as were those from Scalford). However, it closed with the local services in 1953 and the station buildings removed. Remarkably, the station house and cottages have survived despite being empty for many years with the exception of one cottage. The site of the station is now maintained as a grassed area and battery hens are farmed at the goods yard end to the north of the site.

JOHN O'GAUNT

This is probably the only station ever to have been named after a fox covert. Originally it was called Burrow & Twyford, between which two villages the station stood (Burrow is now Burrough) but as there were reports of confusion with Barrow (Lancs) and Twyford (Berks) the name was changed. As place names help to advertise a station, why such an obscure name was chosen is difficult to imagine; the fox covert was only small and 1¹/₂ miles away from the station, near to Marefield Junction. The name was, however, thoroughly approved during 1883 — by the LNWR board in June, the GNR board in July and the Joint Officer's Committee in September!

The buildings were situated on the south side of the road, with the drive to the main building on the Down side. The layout was slightly unusual for the GNR stations as the normal three company cottages were not situated by the drive, but on the main road. These have now been demolished and replaced by one large private house.

The station house, extended and modernised, remains occupied and behind it still stands a building originally erected as a milk processing

Looking north at John O'Gaunt, four months before closure in 1953.
(W. F. Deebank)

Looking in the opposite direction, a class J39 stands at John O'Gaunt in 1957.
(R. Wellings)

Tilton in 1957 viewed in the Melton direction. (R.Wellings)

The main building at Tilton, 1963. (R.Gulliver)

depot. It was in use when the station was at the centre of a large dairy farming area. This building, and one newly built on the site of the station, are now used as industrial premises.

Closure of the station was from 29 April 1957, later than most on the line because a workmen's service to Leicester was retained (just one train in each direction) after the normal local services had stopped.

An unusual occurrence here is that the area close to the station is now called John O'Gaunt after the station, where normally a station was named after the area. It is not unique, however, as the same thing happened, although much earlier and on a larger scale, at Wigston South (Section 2).

TILTON

Had the nearest village been used for the station name it would have been Halstead, but the name of the much larger Tilton prevailed. In fact Tilton villagers had to pass through Halstead, and some way beyond, to reach the station which was in a wide cutting on the north side of the Oakham road.

As it happened, the more popular station for Tilton inhabitants was Lowesby (Section 12) which was almost the same distance from the village, but was more often a better station for the Leicester trains.

After Tilton's 1953 closure for passengers the station was used by the goods yard staff until

East Norton, early this century, looking south. The large station house and cottages can be seen and part of the A47 road bridge shored up.

1963, since when it stood empty until demolished in about 1970. A new house and its garden now stand on the site and still occupied are the adjacent station house and cottages.

EAST NORTON

This station lay in a cutting on the north side of the main A47, ½ mile east of the village. A rather unusual layout was employed as the station drive was on the Down side whilst the main building, including the booking facilities, was opposite. This caused inconvenience to some passengers, but was partly resolved in 1899 when a footpath and steps were provided to give direct access to the Up platform from the road. However, the main intention for its provision was for the benefit of passengers from the Loddington and Belton direction.

Another unusual aspect was the provision of a special wicket gate which allowed direct access to the Up platform solely to Major Haycock, owner of the land through which the railway passed. (A similar privilege was granted to the land owner at Kirby Muxloe.)

Although regular passenger traffic stopped in 1953, a workmen's service was continued to Market Harborough for over four years, the last on 18 May 1957. From then on station buildings gradually became derelict and were removed in the mid 1970s. The cutting has now been infilled and grassed over, but the elegant, LNWR-designed station house and cottages that were built facing the main road remain.

HALLATON

The station house and terrace of railway cottages were situated either side of the line and both can be seen just east of the village on the Horninghold road. Between them were the station buildings on

The buildings were staggered at East Norton (also at Medbourne) as this 1957 view shows. (R. Wellings)

161

The minor building on the Up platform at Hallaton taken in 1948. (R.E. Tustin)

Looking northwards at Hallaton in 1957. (R.Wellings)

Derelict Hallaton in 1971. (R.Gulliver)

Medbourne looking south, taken about the turn of the century. The existing station house can be seen on the right. (Leicestershire Record Office)

In the opposite direction, this photograph of Medbourne was probably taken on completion of the track singling and removal of the Up platform in 1906.

the low embankment where a bungalow now stands. The station drive to the main building was on the Down side and to the same side but further south was another approach from the Medbourne road.

In the early 1970s the station buildings were removed, but there was less to dismantle here than at the other stations — the canopy over the main platform having rotted away long before the regular services finished in 1953 and the workmen's service in 1957.

The station was particularly busy when special services were run on Easter Mondays for the renowned Hallaton versus Medbourne bottle-kicking event. However, these trains were often wrecked by the young passengers and were discontinued in the mid 1920s. Hooliganism on trains apparently is nothing new.

MEDBOURNE

A short distance from Medbourne village in the Uppingham direction the old station drive still leads to the Station Master's house situated low down west of the road overbridge. Nothing else remains on the station site, even the two railway cottages (not of standard design) on the opposite side of the road have been replaced by a new house.

The station was completed with the others on the line in 1879, but not used until the Peterborough service was started from Leicester on 2 July 1883.

Strangely, although this was one of the LNWR-designed stations, its only service was run by the GNR. It was a very meagre service too, and as the curve on which the station stood, between Hallaton and Drayton Junctions, was generally little used, the line was singled in January 1906. Consequently the Up-side platform and building were redundant and removed. (When in use this platform could be reached by steps descending the embankment from the road.) Just over ten years later, from 1 April 1916, the curve was closed completely as a war economy measure and was never reopened.

A fire is said to have destroyed the station building shortly after closure, but the shell at least lingered until removal before the Second World War.

WALTHAM-ON-THE-WOLDS

The intention in building this small station was to run a regular shuttle service from Scalford and it was duly listed in the Great Northern timetable from May 1883. It appeared for 11 successive years, but times for a service were never shown. As far as is known there was never even an experimental service to determine passenger potential.

The only trains to use the station were specials which ran for the Easter race meetings at nearby Croxton Park and for the large Waltham fair and horse sale held each September. The specials were mainly shuttles which met service trains at Scalford, although some were through trains, normally from Leicester and Nottingham. Very rarely trains were run to serve military training camps held at Croxton.

There was just one platform west of the road to Eaton, about 1½ miles north of Waltham. Here the original, single-storey station building still stands and is now converted for use as boarding kennels. It is a plain, rectangular building with pitched roof and next to it once stood a smaller timber structure. Both were normally used for the goods business. On the opposite side of the road a row of cottages still stands, one of which was for the Station Master.

Although essentially at the end of a branch, the station was not truly a dead end as a double track continued for a further ¼ mile beyond the road bridge to allow room for shunting. The special passenger trains were stopped sometime before the last Croxton race meeting in 1913 — perhaps as early as 1903, the year the last train was advertised in the Leicestershire press. Goods traffic stopped officially from 4 May 1964.

Waltham-on-the-Wolds station, about 1930,
looking north-east towards the end of the branch.
(Lens of Sutton)

TILTON TO LEICESTER RAILWAY (GNR)

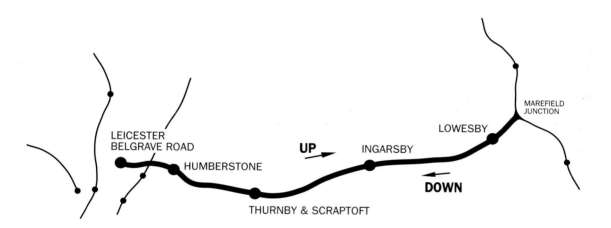

TILTON TO LEICESTER RAILWAY (GNR)

To most local residents this was better known as the line that ran from Belgrave Road station to the Lincolnshire coast holiday resorts. In particular, Skegness was the most popular and this was the destination of the line's first passenger train on 2 October 1882. It was an excursion with almost guaranteed success as similar trips had been regularly run from Melton and Market Harborough on the connecting GN & LNW Joint Line (Section 11) since 1880.

On that opening day from Leicester regular services also started running via Melton Mowbray to meet connecting trains at Harby & Stathern. The only intermediate stops were made on the Joint Line and not at the four stations on this 'Leicester Line' which were not ready for opening until 1 January 1883. Goods trains had been operating since 15 May 1882.

Evident from the stations provided, the Great Northern had great expectations from the line. The stations were well-built, generous structures — particularly at Leicester which turned out to be unnecessarily large. Their architecture was by Henry Fraser who had assisted in engineering the GNR section of the Joint Line, and consequently there were detail similarities in the design of both line's country stations. On this line the stations at Thurnby & Scraptoft, Ingarsby and Lowesby were all virtually identical, but Leicester and Humberstone were quite different.

At the three that were common the main buildings were single-storey and comprised two parallel bays at right-angles to the track, joined by a central section containing the booking hall. Roofs were pitched with raised stone gables on the outer bays, while a recess on the platform side between the bays was covered by a hipped, glazed roof, and this extended by a flat canopy over the platform. Supporting the canopy were four iron columns, their top brackets having a distinctive design incorporating horizontal bar and circles — a stan-

dard of the Great Northern of which similar types could be seen at Redmile and Melton Mowbray. Either side of the canopy were useful draught screens, the tops of their glazed panes curved — matching the heads of all the building's openings.

Standard Great Northern canopy supports at Lowesby.

On the opposite platform, the plain, but large waiting block supported a canopy resembling that on the main building, but was cantilevered only, supported on large brackets that had the prominent sun design like those at the Joint Line stations. Platforms were of concrete.

At all the country stations were other standard buildings: a large station house with distinctive, terra-cotta moulding showing the date of building (1882); square lamp huts with typical pointed roof; and a pair of railway cottages, although at Lowesby there was an additional pair to cater for personnel employed at Marefield Junction.

The Station Masters' houses were similar at each country station. This one survives at Humberstone.

Income from normal passenger trains was very low on this line, especially towards the end of the LNER period as can be seen from the figures in the Appendix. It was freight services that kept the line open for so long, helped by the summer excursion traffic which particularly boosted the income at Leicester Belgrave Road and Humberstone. Although the figures in the Appendix show a high number of season ticket sales on this line they were normally for only one week and therefore had no great effect on revenue.

Regular passenger services were stopped from 7 September 1953, but a workmen's service of one return train per day, calling at all stations, continued until 29 April 1957, and the last excursion — appropriately to Skegness — ran on 9 September 1962. Goods traffic was closed over the line from 1 June 1964, but certain freight trains were able to transfer to the line at Leicester from the Midland Main Line using a spur at Forest Road. This operation ceased from 1 January 1969:

LEICESTER BELGRAVE ROAD

The Great Northern's first intention, at the suggestion of Leicester Corporation, was to build a station in the city jointly with the Midland. The latter though, after much deliberation and showing no enthusiasm to co-operate, considered the idea too expensive, even with sharing the costs. It was a pity for the GNR because the station would have been more convenient for the city centre than the one they were to build which was sited facing Belgrave Road at a point just north of the new Dysart Way, where a super-store now stands.

Belgrave Road station taken shortly before the First War.

A train from Mablethorpe entering the train shed at Belgrave Road in 1961. The large goods warehouse is on the right. (M.A.Cooke)

Because of the protracted negotiations with the Midland the station was not ready when the line was passed for use in September 1882. In order to start revenue-earning services, therefore, temporary wooden waiting rooms and booking office were erected. They were situated on the north side of the platform area and in use for nearly eight months before the building proper was finished.

The usual lay-out for a terminal station was employed with the main building (conveniently at street level) across the head of the buffer stops. There were also waiting rooms and offices along the north side. The structures provided were quite dour, and the station will be remembered more for its colossal trainshed than the buildings' architectural merit.

At the front was a two-storey block with three, pedimented dormer windows — the only worthy features — and either side of the block were plain single-storey bays with pitched roofs. Between the bay to the south and the central section a tower featured, although this was really too squat to be significant. The two-storey section housed the Station Master on the upper floor and over the road-side entrance was attached a large canopy supported on pillars and with glazed, hipped roof. Until its removal around 1950, the canopy at least gave the building some impression of importance.

On the platform side a large clock overlooked the concourse behind the buffer stops and beneath it at one time a handbell was located. This was rung five minutes before the departure of regular trains (a common occurrence at larger GNR stations)

Boards covering the track on the northern side of the station where parcels traffic was handled. (B.J.Smith)

and very often by young children at other times as well. Facilities included a bookstall until 1916 and refreshment room until the 1920s.

Most impressive was the double-span, arched roof of the trainshed. It was of slate and glass and reminiscent of a small King's Cross without the end screens. It covered about half the length of the long and very wide platforms — six in all, although the outer ones ran only a short distance under cover. A similar, but much shorter arched

roof was attached to the south side of the train-shed. It covered an area from where light goods were dispatched.

Originally there was a ticket platform situated about ¼ mile from the station — just beyond Catherine Street bridge. It probably saw little use for regular traffic though, as tickets from the relatively few passengers could have been collected just as easily at the station which had few exits.

Passenger departures and arrivals were normally conducted from platforms 4 and 5. These were latterly separated by a low screen from the platforms on the north side of the station where the more-important small goods business was carried out. Even much of the track in platform 2 was boarded over to create extra room for goods handling.

By providing such a large station the GNR certainly intended to make a good impression, but it served few routes and never fulfilled expectations. By 1953, when services were reduced to only one weekday train each way, it was described as being the largest station with the smallest service in the country.

Long before this, buildings were under-utilised and some had been let out for various businesses. During the war it was even a base for the home guard. Occupiers over the years included roofing and electrical contractors, an animal feed manufacturer, car sales, and finally a scrap-metal merchant who took over the whole site before the buildings were demolished in 1972.

HUMBERSTONE

An angled bridge took the line over Uppingham Road, Leicester between Lynton Road and The Martival, with the station sited on the high embankment just north of the bridge. The main building stood on the Down side fronted by a tri-

*An external view of disused
Humberstone taken from
Uppingham Road in 1963.
(V.Millington)*

Unusually, more adults than children wait at Humberstone for the special train to the East Coast in 1957. (W.F.Deebank)

Looking east at Humberstone station, about 1957. (R.Wellings)

angular forecourt (which became the site of a petrol station and subsequently a dry-cleaners) at the side of which can still be seen the Station Master's house – almost opposite St Barnabas Road.

Although on an embankment with lightweight timber platforms, buildings were of brick and their foundations solidly built up from ground level. The minor building stood on arched pillars, but the other building was effectively two-storey, with a ground floor that contained an office, coal store and main entrance which was enhanced with pedimented decoration in brick. From here an internal staircase led to the booking office at high level.

To reach the opposite platform, an inclined path ascended the embankment from the road — originally a steep flight of steps was used. The path ran behind the station signal box, a structure that appeared to be precariously balanced between the platform end and the bridge abutments. Because of the station's elevated position, building costs

were much higher than for the line's three conventional stations — £2220 compared with £1580.

At platform level both buildings appeared as rectangular blocks with pitched roofs, each having a high, glazed ventilator above the conveniences and cantilevered awning over the platform. Their last use was for the trains to the coast in 1962 and buildings removed completely five years later. From the Second World War supervision of the station was conducted from Thurnby & Scraptoft.

The two railway cottages which stood opposite the station at the corner of Kitchener Road were demolished in the early 1970s, whilst the station embankment was removed for industrial development in 1981.

THURNBY & SCRAPTOFT

This was one of the line's standard stations located west of an overbridge on the Thurnby to Scraptoft road. The station drive on the Down side is no longer passable, but the site can be reached

A road side view of Thurnby & Scraptoft with station house in 1961.
(B.J. Smith)

A Leicester-bound train entering Thurnby & Scraptoft early this century.

from Telford Way in the housing estate that now surrounds the area. The station was also approachable from the main road by steps ascending the embankment on the Up side.

Although the station buildings have been removed, the two cottages remain by the former drive and facing them can still be seen the Station Master's house. This is hardly recognisable now as it has the unusual distinction of being converted into a pair of shops. The fact that two premises could be made from one shows just how large the station houses were. Additional shops have been built onto its south side and it is now part of a shopping centre.

Soon after the station's opening, an unusual request was sent to the Railway Company from the residents of Thurnby. Because of their strong religious beliefs they asked for the Sunday services at the station to be withdrawn forthwith. Fortunately for many excursionists who used the station on the Sabbath (including the last in 1962) they did not succeed.

The station returns in the Appendix show how very poorly this station was supported towards the end of the 1930s — no doubt the local bus service was a far more convenient alternative.

Hollyhocks in profusion at Thurnby & Scraptoft taken from the west side in 1957. (R.Wellings)

INGARSBY

Midway between the villages of Houghton-on-the-Hill and Hungarton, the road ran beneath the line and then for a short distance parallel to it. Here the station was located, the main building on the Up side and station house almost next to it. Both platforms could also be approached by separate drives, either side of the line, from the Billesdon to Keyham road to the east. On the drive to the Down side the station cottages can still be seen.

The goods yard and regular passenger trains both finished in December 1953 and so during the time of the workmen's service this station was run as an unstaffed halt. This also applied to Lowesby.

After stopping of the workmen's service in 1957 this rural station fell into disrepair and the Down platform building was removed. Fortunately, in the 1960s the main building was purchased and renovated as a dwelling with the station character

retained. The station house, with only slight alterations, is also occupied.

The hamlet of Ingarsby was very sparsely populated and so from the start the station was timetabled 'for', or 'station for' Houghton, a far larger village nearly two miles to the south. This lasted until 1955 when the suffix was dropped. There was also a change in 1939 from Ingersby to Ingarsby, albeit rather late as the normal spelling of the village with an 'a' had generally been used from about 40 years earlier.

LOWESBY

The station drive from the main road is extremely long here — nearly ¼ mile — but why is uncertain. Maybe it was to avoid building in the cutting by the road, or possibly to give a shorter journey to passengers walking from the two nearest villages, Lowesby and Tilton-on-the-Hill, who could use the more direct footpaths to the station across open

Ingarsby in Edwardian times when striped valances were still in vogue.

Ingarsby with a class J6 working 'wrong line' towards Leicester in 1947. (National Railway Museum)

Looking eastward at the well-tended Lowesby station early in the 1950s. (W.F. Deebank)

fields. The drive branches from the main road between the two villages and ran along the south side of the line.

In one way it was a pity the station was not nearer the road as more people could have seen the magnificent floral displays that appeared in the platform gardens for many years. There were similar displays at Thurnby & Scraptoft, great rivals in the inter-station garden contests, but more prizes were won by Lowesby!

When the line was built, the village spelling was 'Loseby' and the station timetabled as this until December 1916 when 'Lowesby', the village's preferred spelling, was used. Of note from the station statistics in the Appendix is how much parcel business was generated from such a rural area.

On the station's closure in 1957 a scrap dealer used the site, followed by a coal merchant. Both have used the standard-pattern platform buildings for storage, but the buildings are now quite derelict and, regretfully, appear to be beyond repair. Remaining virtually as built are the four railway cottages and station house at the side of the very long drive.

The ornate brackets are apparent at derelict Lowesby in 1982.

173

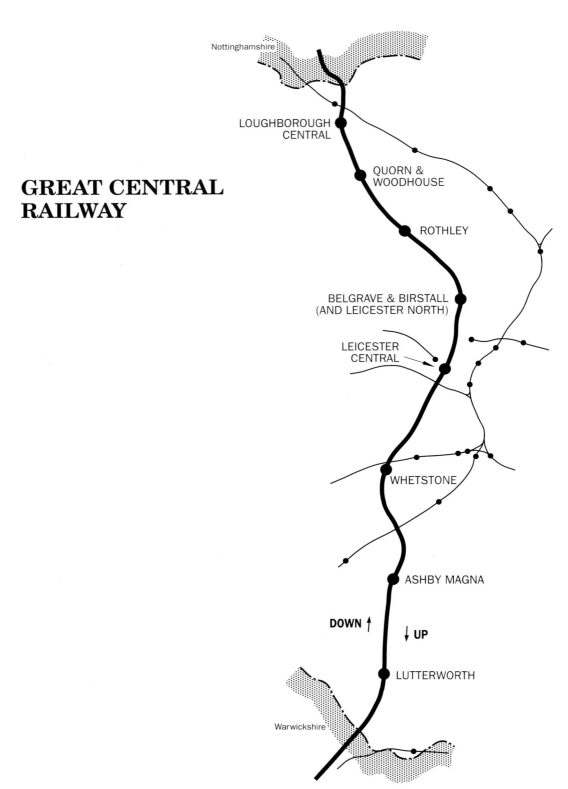

**GREAT CENTRAL
RAILWAY**

Nottinghamshire

LOUGHBOROUGH
CENTRAL

QUORN &
WOODHOUSE

ROTHLEY

BELGRAVE & BIRSTALL
(AND LEICESTER NORTH)

LEICESTER
CENTRAL

WHETSTONE

ASHBY MAGNA

DOWN ↑   ↓ UP

LUTTERWORTH

Warwickshire

GREAT CENTRAL RAILWAY

Now renowned for its locally preserved section, this former main line was provided with eight stations in Leicestershire, all opening with the line on 15 March 1899. Six days earlier specials had run to the opening ceremony at Marylebone and coal trains were first moved on 25 July the previous year.

The basic design for these high quality stations was by the Great Central's Chief Engineer Alexander Ross, but with detail changes and the larger Loughborough and Leicester stations by the line's Resident Engineer Edward Parry. All eight were built on the efficient island principle, saving the duplication of buildings and staff, and also allowing for the easy quadrupling of tracks that was envisaged on this line. A disadvantage was that steps were always necessary to reach the platforms — rather inconvenient with heavy luggage — although lifts were provided at Loughborough and Leicester.

At these last two other differences made them quite special and so are described individually, but at each of the country stations facilities were very similar, particularly on the platforms, where there was always three basic buildings. These comprised a square block with booking office and Station Master's office; rectangular block containing general and ladies waiting rooms; and at the end, a rather draughty gentlemen's convenience block with open roof.

The buildings were by no means plain. Roofs on the first two blocks were pitched with raised stone gables, the gable ends showing a stepped pattern relief, whilst string courses of Derbyshire gritstone were included above and below the square-headed windows. A short awning, originally glazed, protected the platform between the staircase and booking office with the valance on the awning similarly profiled at each station. Mention must also be made of the signs on the buildings as they were so distinctive in embellished cast iron and peculiar to the stations on this main line.

At four of the small stations the platform was reached from a road overbridge through a gated, arched entrance and by descending a covered staircase. Examples can still be seen at the preserved Quorn & Woodhouse and Rothley stations — Belgrave & Birstall and Ashby Magna being the other two. With this type of approach there was

Typical cast-iron sign used on stations of the London extension.

The arched entrance to Rothley station - a standard style where access is from a road over-bridge.

space beneath the staircase and within the bridge abutment for small rooms used by porters and for storage.

At Whetstone and Lutterworth the platforms were at high level and reached by a staircase that ascended from an arched entrance beneath a road under-bridge. On the platform a glazed, flat-roofed structure covered the stairwell, whilst for the porters a separate block was provided on the side of the road-bridge opposite to the platform.

This latter type of approach was also planned for an 'excursion platform' at the southern end of Swithland reservoir. Day-trippers were to be the main users at this delightful part of the County, but with Rothley station less than a mile to the south its

building was never justified. Nevertheless, the tracks were still laid out ready to take the island platform and signs of the halt's prospective entrance can still be seen within the bridge that spans the road between Swithland and Rothley.

Well-built structures were also provided for housing the Station Masters. All were to a common design except at Loughborough and Leicester where existing and more substantial accommodation was used. The GCR-designed houses all remain except at Ashby Magna.

Although most were similarly housed, the Station Masters, as far as passenger numbers were concerned, had varying amounts of responsibility. This is revealed in the only known records of individual

*The entrance from road level to the proposed Swithland station.
(Leicestershire Record Office)*

The large station house at Whetstone with modern additions.

station ticket receipts that have survived for this line in Great Central days. They are from three complete years, 1917-19:

	1917	1918	1919
Loughborough	£11,302	£15,260	£18,977
Quorn & Woodhouse	£3,505	£4,113	£5,094
Rothley	£3,933	£4,653	£6,000
Belgrave & Birstall	£920	£989	£1,294
Leicester	£37,853	£50,622	£67,266
Whetstone	£1,802	£2,358	£2,563
Ashby Magna	£1,470	£1,919	£2,390
Lutterworth	£3,710	£4,731	£5,762

Of note from these figures is how receipts increased substantially during the three years — no doubt the cessation of the First World War had a marked effect. (Incidently, the receipts at the Loughborough station were approximately three quarters of those at Loughborough Midland for the same three years.)

Further figures from the LNER period of ownership can be seen in the Appendix. They show clearly the effects that road transport had on the line between the periods shown, especially at Quorn & Woodhouse, Rothley and Whetstone where bookings fell by approximately three-quarters in 13 years. Also notable is that receipts from season tickets were once high indicating that this had been a commuter line.

But by the time of the Beeching closures even commuters were few. Firstly, four stations — Quorn & Woodhouse, Rothley, Belgrave & Birstall

and Whetstone — were closed to passengers from 4 March 1963 despite a strong campaign by Lord Lanesborough of Swithland Hall to have them turned into halts. Following this all goods traffic on the line was finished from 14 June 1965 and when through trains to London were discontinued from 5 September 1966, the remaining stations (between Rugby and Arkwright Street, Nottingham) were reduced to unstaffed halts. Complete closure, as far as British Railways was concerned, came less than three years later — from 5 May 1969.

Since then remarkable achievements by dedicated preservationists have ensured that the main line lives on. Regular trips were again running from Loughborough to Quorn & Woodhouse on 23 March 1974; as far as Rothley on 3 January 1976; and to the site of Belgrave & Birstall station on 18 November 1990. Thankfully, through the persistence of hard-working volunteers, the three most northerly of the eight County stations have been expertly preserved, virtually as originally built:

LOUGHBOROUGH CENTRAL

Loughborough's Great Central Road, newly built with the line, provides access to the station which is entered from a road overbridge directly into the booking hall. The building at this level features opening surrounds and string courses of Derbyshire gritstone, and supports an unusual double-ridged roof. Spanning the front of the building is a distinctive awning, comprising three, deep glazed ridges. Inside, a striking mass of var-

The booking office entrance at Loughborough taken in 1992.

Loughborough Central, the Down-side platform buildings in 1983.

The north end of Loughborough Central platforms in 1951. (National Railway Museum)

nished teak panelling fronts the booking office on one side of the hall and former parcels and luggage offices on the other.

The platforms are reached by a wide stairway, covered and glazed, and an interesting remnant at one side of the steps is a long grooved board once used to ease the wheeling of cycles. Passenger facilities (that include amongst the normal ones a refreshment room, with cellars beneath and rooms formerly for first-class passengers) are contained in two, long blocks that run along the centre of the island platform — a small third block is for the gent's convenience. Platform protection is plentiful with glazed awnings of the ridge and furrow type, mostly cantilevered from the two main blocks.

Beneath the level of the booking hall are rooms once used by the porters, and at the east side of the stairway evidence of an added lift shaft can be seen. This was for a new lift provided in the early 1950s, but it was in use for less than 20 years before the machinery was moved to Burton-on-Trent.

Since takeover by the Main Line Steam Trust — the body which runs the preserved section of railway — the station has been excellently renovated, in particular the woodwork in the booking hall and in the waiting rooms. Other rooms have been converted for the sale of books and souvenirs. The only other significant alteration is at the base of the lift shaft where an entrance has been made to a splendid museum that extends beneath the booking hall.

One connection with the station which has not survived is the station house. This was a grand villa, not built by the railway, but purchased especially for the Station Master. It was situated east of the station between Little Moor Lane and the Empress Road bridge.

QUORN & WOODHOUSE

According to an agreement with the local landowning family (the Farnhams) at the time of construction, this station should never have closed — for in return for permission to build, the GCR

A class B1 about to pass Quorn & Woodhouse in 1959 en route to Manchester. (M.A.Cooke)

Derelict Quorn & Woodhouse in 1969. (John Bailey)

pledged that a service to the station would be maintained forever. However, as British Railways made clear when this point was raised at the time of closure in 1963, there would be difficulty in maintaining a service when the rest of the line was closed down. Now in preservation, the station's perpetuity is far more assured.

Although the design is standard, visitors may notice the unusual, predominantly blue colour scheme. This is to recreate the appearance that a few LNER stations took in pre-war days. Incidentally, a detailed painting specification that has survived for the London extension stations shows that in early GCR days the metalwork was in two shades of blue, excepting lamps and guttering in red, whilst doors and valences were in two shades of oak. The stations must have been very attractive.

Being in the centre of prime hunting country, famous faces were to pass through the station. One was the Prince of Wales, later King Edward VIII, who apparently used the station's ticket office to change out of his riding habit.

Like most stations on the Great Central's London extension, this one served only a small population, lying between the villages of Quorn and diminutive Woodhouse, although it was handy for recreational visits by Leicester people to the countryside — in particular to Woodhouse Eaves. Between the Wars it became of limited use for the local population who were finding road transport more convenient for commuting. From about 1930 the station's administration was combined with Rothley.

Rothley, taken soon after opening, looking northwards.

ROTHLEY

When plans of the line were first issued Rothley residents were appalled that land had been allowed for a station at neighbouring Swithland but not for their own village. However, strong representation to the Railway Company, especially from Lord of the Manor, Frederick Merttens, eventually swayed things their way, and to the detriment of Swithland a station was allocated midway between Rothley and Cropston. Another reason Swithland may not have been chosen was because the Earl of Lanesborough, some of whose land the railway had purchased, had insisted that he could stop any train he wished at Swithland — which was not, of course, in the railway's interest.

The site chosen for the station turned out to be of great interest to archaeologists because, during excavation, not only was evidence of an Anglo Saxon burial ground found, but also the discovery of a Roman settlement. Perhaps disturbance of the former has something to do with the belief that the station is haunted.

In LNER days the platform canopies at the other country stations were replaced by a shallow-pitched type in asbestos, but the one here must have been more robust and has survived in the original glazed, double-ridged form. It recently though, has required much renovation.

Features which have fortunately survived into preservation are the welcoming coal fires in the general waiting room — always lit on cold winter days (also at Quorn & Woodhouse) — and the gas lighting which gives the station a special atmosphere after dark. Electricity was not run to this station until well after BR days.

Modern platform scene at Rothley in 1993.

Beneath the stairs an excellent, small museum representing an old parcels office has been created, and the ladies waiting room has been converted for serving refreshments. The only other major change is the re-siting of the station signal box (now one transferred from Blind Lane) to a point opposite the Down platform, the original site being some 200 yards further south.

BELGRAVE & BIRSTALL AND LEICESTER NORTH

A new road was specially made to access Belgrave & Birstall station from the main A6, the road also providing access to the Birstall Golf Club. The road was probably used more by the club though, than the station, for the latter was little used — not surprising as after the early years both Birstall and Belgrave residents could more conveniently catch a bus or tram for the short journey to Leicester, their usual destination.

However, the station was also intended to serve as a ticket collecting platform for Leicester Central and for this reason an extra free-standing office was provided for the ticket examiners. It was situated between the waiting block and gent's convenience. For how long the office was used is not certain — perhaps not at all — as there is a record of ticket collectors being employed at Leicester from its opening. A possibility, to start with at least, is that Leicester collected from Down trains only as there was no collector's office at the first station south of Leicester. The office at Belgrave & Birstall was latterly used by the Station Master.

Goods facilities were not available here — there was little room with the station in a deep cutting — and coal (also originally livestock) was handled at a large depot just over a mile to the south at Abbey Lane which served the areas north of Leicester.

Belgrave & Birstall from the south, about 1910. Great Central coaches, ticket collector's building and golf clubhouse can be seen.

A view taken two days before closure in 1963. (H.W.Sadler)

The southern terminus of the preserved railway at Birstall called Leicester North.

After station closure in 1963, buildings gradually fell into disrepair and were badly vandalised. They were in such a poor state that when the pre-served line's southern extension was planned it was decided to raze the buildings completely and, as there were already two stations of similar design, to eventually rebuild in a different but fit-ting style. The entrance arch on the road-bridge was bricked up (and remains so) and the platform buildings demolished in 1977.

Four years later the platforms were removed when site clearance was under way for the rail-way's new terminus (Leicester North) just to the south of the old station. So far, a long platform on the Down side has been provided, passengers able to board trains for the first time at its ceremonial opening on 5 July 1991. A short platform was also built on the opposite side allowing stabling room for a coach that is used as a temporary ticket office.

When funds allow this platform will be fully extended and a new station building constructed. As it is a terminal station the design proposed is a two-storey edifice in late Victorian style appropri-ately with strong similarities to Marylebone, com-plete with iron and glass canopies. (Fittingly the buffer stops already used at the station are ones transferred from Marylebone.) Like grand station buildings of the past, the new one should form a major part in advertising and promoting the rail-way. Entrance to the new site is from 'The Sidings' on Leicester's northern ring road.

Two incidental notes — the proposed building will be virtually on the site of a large blacksmith's workshop, used by contractors during the line's construction, and to the east of the intended build-ing the original station house can still be seen, coincidentally much nearer to the new station than the original.

LEICESTER CENTRAL

As early as 1890, during the line's original plan-ning, attempts were made by the Company Chairman, Sir Edward Watkin, and Leicester Corporation to interest the Midland, LNWR and Great Northern Companies in providing a joint station that was central to the town. However, the Midland and its partner in Leicester, the LNWR, did not wish to co-operate with their great rival to London and the Great Northern also refused the invitation having built its own terminal in Belgrave Road not many years before.

So Watkin had to go it alone, expensively clear-ing away numerous small dwellings, re-housing the occupants and severing many side roads on the west side of the town to fit in the elevated sta-tion. Fortunately for the railway, the Leicester Corporation were very accommodating and even paid for the construction of Great Central Street on which the large station frontage was built. One property which was not moved though, was an important piece of Roman mosaic pavement which was housed beneath the station. Access to it was maintained for visitors from a special entrance at the rear.

The frontage of Leicester Central in 1899 before installation of the clock face.

Delays on building the station were frequent and contributed to holding up the line's opening for passengers by several months. Even on the opening day parts of the platform buildings and much of the frontage were still not finished. However, when completed, the frontage was imposing with strong similarities to Leicester London Road in design and treatment — but unfortunately here, with its cramped surroundings, the elevation could not be appreciated from a distance.

In the long facade were three sets of wrought-iron gates — allowing access for vehicles into a huge carriage area — and two smaller gates for pedestrians. Between them were many windows, mostly in pairs, their round heads divided by radial sections of stone, a trait repeated for virtually all openings (and blind arcading) throughout the ground floor and platform buildings.

The parapet was particularly ornate, formed of nine decorated Dutch gables with urns between, and perched centrally amongst them a clock tower in Baroque style that dominated the facade. Much decoration was in Yorkshire stone and buff terracotta from Hathern, the materials most noticeable over a separate gateway that still exists at the southern end, where in large letters is announced the entrance to the Parcels Offices.

Behind the facade ran the glass-roofed carriage/cab area that became primarily used for car parking. From a central point in here passengers entered the booking hall with booking office on the right and parcels office opposite — this latter office at the end of a large two-storey building that extended southwards behind the carriage area and dealt generally with the small goods business. The top of this building can still be seen

A poster for the World Cup (1966) dates this view of the dingy booking hall at Leicester. The right-hand tunnel once led to the northern end of the platform. (A. Sanderson)

*The top of the south stair
at Leicester Central.
(A.Sanderson)*

*The bookstall at
Leicester Central in 1966.
(A.Sanderson)*

from former platform level and is noticeable for its Dutch gables (matching those on the facade) a style occasionally favoured by the Great Central in its days as the Manchester Sheffield & Lincolnshire Railway before 1897.

At the end of the booking hall three rather dingy tunnels, barrel vaulted and lined with white, glazed bricks, passed beneath the tracks. The middle one led to a luggage lift, whilst the outer ones led passengers, via stairs, to respective north or south sections of the island platform. At one time the tunnels could be approached from a small entrance between the arches at the rear of the station.

At platform level the stairwells were guarded by spiked railings and barrier gates where the ticket collectors stood. In latter years only the south stair was used, this side facing a large Smith's bookstall. (Originally the bookstall was in the booking hall.)

Along the platform the single-storey buildings were arranged with one block south of the stairs and two blocks to the north. These contained the usual staff offices, rooms for both class of passengers, a refreshment and dining room. The latter was particularly renowned, said to be of such high standard that at one time was second best only to Leicester's Grand Hotel, and often used by town

The platform for London in LNER days at Leicester Central. (Stations U.K.)

folk who were not necessarily travelling by rail. It retained a grand Victorian character to its end in 1951, being richly decorated with the likes of American walnut panelling, embossed glazed tiles and velvet curtains.

The kitchens were at ground level, food and drinks reaching the upper level by a service lift. Also down below were the staff mess rooms — reached by a separate staircase from the platform — and at one time a bakery from which bread was supplied to catering establishments on all parts of the Great Central system.

The main station platforms were very long, virtually ¼ mile, ample for the longest mainline trains and in the early years sufficient to accommodate two formations. On these occasions, to enable one train to arrive or depart while another

was at the same platform, central scissor points were used (similar to the original arrangement at Leicester Campbell Street) with control from a platform signal box situated at the top of the northern stairwell. When taken out of use the box was employed by the transport police. Two-road bays each end of the station accommodated local Nottingham and Rugby trains until 1959, and on the Down bay platform at the southern end stood a tall ventilator and an inset glazed section, both for the benefit of the vault housing the Roman pavement beneath.

With the exception of the ends of the bays, the whole platform area was covered by a vast expanse of glazed, ridged canopies, hipped at the ends and supported by extensive lattice girders resting on rows of cast-iron and fabricated pillars. A bright and airy platform was created with clear

The south bay platform with a 'Black 5' and a Bournemouth-bound type 3 diesel in the Up platform at Leicester. The top floor of the building for handling small goods can be seen on the right. (K. Lane)

The former Line-Engineer's office and Station Master's house in Talbot Lane Leicester.

was a gradual run down of services and after serving almost three years as an unstaffed halt (said to be the largest unstaffed halt in the country, excepting the lady in the bookstall) closure came in 1969. Two years later the platform and its substantial buildings were removed having been in use for only 70 years.

The large elevated area has been turned into a car park and siting for industrial units. The parcels offices, booking hall and carriage area, including some of its iron gates, remain and the buildings are now mostly used by motor traders. The Roman pavement was moved to the nearby Jewry Wall museum in 1977.

Also to be seen, not far from the station, is the house used by the Station Master until the Second World War. It was formerly the engineer's offices during construction of the station and is a delightful Georgian house situated at 12 Talbot Lane.

WHETSTONE

This was a conventional London extension station as described at the start of the section. Access was from beneath the rail bridge which once spanned Station Street near the centre of the village. The platform was on the south side of the bridge on an embankment that was particularly wide to accommodate the goods yard.

Since the station's 1963 closure this embankment has been removed, along with all station buildings, to make way for new houses but the large station house remains just east of the station site.

views of parts of city and county — although at this elevation passengers were always at the mercy of the wind.

The only alteration of any note was to the frontage in 1957 — during the line's declining years. To avoid spending money on repairs the whole of the parapet and clock tower were removed and replaced by an incompatible, plain brick wall. It was obvious from this sort of treatment which way the station was heading. There

The Down platform at Whetstone at the beginning of its life. (Leicestershire Record Office)

Whetstone, little changed, at the end of its life, looking north.

ASHBY MAGNA

This was a standard style of country station that served mainly Dunton Bassett and Ashby Magna and was situated midway between the two villages on the south side of the road. It appears there were many commuters from the villages who started their journey on cycles as, in addition to the standard buildings on the platform, a lengthy cycle shed was at one time provided between the waiting block and gent's convenience.

No doubt the few commuters from Ashby Magna remaining in the early 1960s were inconvenienced when the M1 motorway was being constructed on the east side of the station. Its building entailed re-alignment of the road between the station and Ashby and also re-positioning of the drive to the goods sidings — although these were little used at

this time. Unfortunately, the Station Master's house was at the entrance of this drive and had to be demolished.

Seemingly no busier than the other small stations on the line, this station was able to survive the line's initial round of passenger closures of 1963; it may have been because a replacement bus service was not proposed as required by law. More surprising is that the station was given an extra service when the stations between Nottingham and Rugby became unstaffed halts in 1966. All service trains were then stopping at the station, but this luxury lasted only until 1969 when the line closed.

All traces of the station have now disappeared including the wall that contained the passenger

Railway staff of varying grades taken at Ashby Magna shortly after opening.

Looking south at Ashby Magna, about 1962. (Les Hales)

gateway on the road overbridge. This was removed with recent strengthening of the bridge. A timber company currently operates from the station site.

LUTTERWORTH

Lutterworth residents had relied on two remote stations for a long time: Ullesthorpe, for nearly 60 years (three miles distant and regularly served by horse-bus) and Welford & Kilworth (five miles away) which had been used for nearly 50 years.

But the Great Central arrived and built a prominent station on an embankment immediately east of the town centre. (The Midland Railway must have missed the Lutterworth traffic at Ullesthorpe, for in 1901 they lent a horse bus to a local carrier in the hope of ferrying Leicester and Rugby bound passengers to their own station.)

The new station was similar to Whetstone with the island platform reached from a road underbridge, but here the platform continued over the bridge and buildings, except the porter's block, were on the northern side. The bridge was actually built as a means of access to the station rather than to span an existing road.

Different to the line's other small stations, the station approach was not used to access the goods yard. Instead there was a separate approach road further to the north.

On the platform, the glass-roofed canopy was an extended version of the normal type for country stations with intermediate pillar supports and, for reasons unknown, when the canopy was rebuilt in LNER days, the decorated valances were omitted from the front edges. Perhaps because of the station's

With Station Master in tails and an army officer on the platform, perhaps an important visitor was awaited at Lutterworth, about 1912. (K.Deacon)

Looking south at Lutterworth two months before closure in 1969. (Andrew Muckley)

A view in the same year showing the site of the goods yard, the glazed structure above the stair-well and an unusual conversion of gas to electric lamp. (Andrew Muckley)

exposed position, a large protective screen was installed at one side of the booking window and, similar to Ashby Magna, a cycle shed was provided on the platform. In its early days the station was busy enough to support a W.H.Smith bookstall.

Since the 1969 closure and demolition of everything except the bridge, the embankment has been left untouched and overgrown, leaving the bricked-up entrance in the bridge virtually the only sign of the station. The station house, surrounded by tall trees, lies to the front of the station site.

APPENDIX

STATION TRAFFIC RETURNS

Individual traffic returns — including number of passengers booked, passenger receipts and number of season tickets issued — exist for nearly all stations of the Midland Railway between the years 1872 and 1922. Of the other pre-grouping companies only a relatively few have survived and these are included in the text of their respective section. From the post-grouping days individual figures are available for certain stations of the LNER between 1923 and 1938, but the whereabouts of all British Railways' returns are unknown — if they survive at all.

The Midland returns constitute a mass of figures — rather too many for all to be reproduced, and so representative samples have been extracted, sufficient it is hoped to allow useful analysis. The samples are taken from four, separate, three-year periods (where possible 1872-4, 1888-90, 1905-7, 1920-2) and for each period the annual, average figures have been calculated. This allows easy comparison of station returns. (Season tickets were not recorded by the Midland for the period 1872-83.)

The figures clearly show how the Midland's stations grew — but the sometimes dramatic decreases that occured under grouped and nationalised ownership unfortunately cannot be illustrated without all the traffic returns.

Figures of the LNER that have survived include those from stations of the former GN & LNW Joint Railway (Section 11), former Great Northern (Section 12) and former Great Central (section 13). The samples used are tabulated, like the Midland's, in three-year periods and show the annual, average returns for the years 1923-5 and 1936-8. With the LNER figures the income from season tickets was recorded separately allowing comparison of income from normal bookings. Also tabulated, where available, is the income from parcels handled on passenger trains. The figures are taken from the middle of the LNER era to give a brief insight into how important this revenue was compared with that from passenger traffic.

To be noted is that although returns for a particular station may have been low, the station could have been one of importance and quite busy. This would occur if many of the passengers were visitors or just changing trains and booking from another station.

From the amount of passengers booked and receipts, approximate average prices paid per ticket can be calculated — results indicating predominantly long or short journeys from a station. With the Midland figures they can only be approximate because the receipts include season ticket sales for which allowance has to be made. Journeys using season tickets could equate to between approximately 24 and 160 bookings depending whether they were for one, three or six months — their usual durations. A variation in sales of season tickets is an important factor when studying increase or decrease in passengers booking at a station.

With the traffic returns of the Midland stations are samples of weekly timetabled departures, the figures again helping to indicate how stations compared (the LNER weekly departures are not included because of the complexity with conditional stops and seasonal variances). Two separate periods have been chosen, 1905-7 and 1920-2 (periods when departures were at their height) and by using the number of passengers booked during these years, it has been convenient to calculate — approximately — the average number of booked passengers that boarded each train.

With passenger figures unavailable from the 1960s — during the time of widespread closures — it is unfortunate that similar calculations are not possible so that comparisons could be made of stations during their busiest and (possibly) lowest periods of use.

SECTION 1
LEICESTER & SWANNINGTON RAILWAY AND LEICESTER & BURTON BRANCH

		a passengers booked / b passenger receipts (incl. season tickets) / c season tickets (annual averages from 3-year periods)				d weekly train departures / e average booked passengers boarding each train (excluding season ticket holders)	
		1872-4	1888-90	1905-7	1920-2	1905-7	1920-2
Leicester (West Bridge)	a	16274	22759	24389	25745	d 13	12
	b	£386	£406	£469	£687	e 36.0	41.3
	c	-	5	4	6		
Glenfield	a	4147	12859	13932	17235	d 26	24
	b	£65	£245	£355	£446	e 10.3	13.8
	c	-	3	35	42		
Ratby	a	4304	10810	11615	9904	d 26	24
	b	£94	£278	£276	£616	e 8.6	7.9
	c	-	5	15	76		
Desford	a	15252	20903	28334	27628	d 137	115
	b	£831	£1057	£1628	£3595	e 4.0	4.6
	c	-	29	60	136		
Bagworth & Ellistown	a	17090	20210	37575	46201	d 101	103
	b	£1039	£1322	£2251	£7177	e 7.2	8.6
	c	-	5	19	343		
Bardon Hill	a	6861	9007	14514	19876	d 101	103
	b	£439	£440	£866	£2586	e 2.8	3.7
	c	-	3	16	93		
Coalville Town	a	44175	57444	116861	124073	d 224*	108
	b	£2610	£3409	£7424	£18310	e 10.0	22.1
	c	-	11	97	730		
Swannington	a	9731	11275	18517	26493	d 92	82
	b	£358	£351	£501	£1952	e 3.9	6.2
	c	-	2	12	152		
Ashby-de-la-Zouch **	a	83788	91430	108769	117170	d 242*	166*
	b	£4333	£1603	£6592	£12211	e 8.6	13.6
	c	-	21	75	222		
Moira	a	43213	42926	56958	67584	d 232*	160*
	b	£1098	£982	£2087	£4968	e 7	8.1
	c	-	3	38	144		
Kirby Muxloe	a	5365	10915	27446	23147	d 128	103
	b	£180	£506	£1615	£3108	e 4.1	4.3
	c	-	42	118	265		

* including Ashby-Nuneaton Joint line trains
** including branch platform on Derby line

		a passengers booked				d weekly train departures	
		b passenger receipts (incl. season tickets)				e average booked passengers boarding each train (excluding season ticket holders)	
		c season tickets					
		(annual averages from 3-year periods)					
		1872-4	1888-90	1905-7	1920-2	1905-7	1920-2
Loughborough	a	116978	156810	167282	199001	d 330	239
	b	£9402	£13463	£16528	£35024	e 9.7	16.0
	c	-	73	203	513		
Barrow-on-Soar	a	38151	46617	68474	94827	d 174	150
	b	£1650	£1836	£2389	£6383	e 7.6	12.2
	c	-	19	125	502		
Sileby	a	28569	40187	68243	87967	d 162	156
	b	£1117	£1551	£2661	£8123	e 8.1	10.8
	c	-	40	144	480		
Syston	a	54676	79086	89415	111132	d 328	293
	b	£2502	£3676	£4641	£11581	e 5.2	7.3
	c	-	208	571	1106		
Humberstone Road	a	47633*	53078	33991	17063	d 256	155
	b	£1942*	£2199	£1551	£1616	e 2.6	2.1
	c	-	26	49	60		
Leicester	a	481101	597769	686554	887945	d 769	573
	b	£66543	£86637	£118589	£304981	e 17.2	29.8
	c	-	254	753	1756		
Wigston South	a	8254	38800	44350	49315	d 118	76
	b	£199	£877	£1795	£3504	e 7.2	12.5
	c	-	59	173	109		
Countesthorpe	a	15984	18989	18084	21594	d 76	76
	b	£501	£663	£816	£1992	e 4.6	5.5
	c	-	14	74	134		
Broughton Astley	a	13072	16692	13764	13266	d 76	76
	b	£662	£858	£835	£2304	e 3.5	3.4
	c	-	12	27	156		
Ullesthorpe	a	19123	23517	13517	11729	d 76	70
	b	£1408	£1749	£1015	£1875	e 3.4	3.2
	c	-	5	20	67		

* 1876-8 instead of 1872-4 (station opened 1875)

SECTION 3
SYSTON & PETERBOROUGH RAILWAY

		a passengers booked b passenger receipts (incl. season tickets) c season tickets (annual averages from 3-year periods)				d weekly train departures e average booked passengers boarding each train (excluding season ticket holders)	
		1872-4	1888-90	1905-7	1920-2	1905-7	1920-2
Rearsby	a b c	8237 £278 -	14242 £595 7	17612 £841 35	17936 £2061 121	d 124 e 2.7	107 3.2
Brooksby	a b c	9003 £458 -	12051 £626 8	12072 £765 22	11890 £1461 48	d 124 e 1.9	113 2.0
Frisby	a b c	4567 £147 -	6671 £238 6	8897 £352 8	9188 £957 50	d 118 e 1.4	100 1.8
Asfordby	a b c	6219 £324 -	6688 £228 2	12967 £682 15	15686 £1226 41	d 118 e 2.1	100 3.0
Melton Mowbray	a b c	49854 £5968 -	56351 £5955 53	88315 £9954 66	107700 £21566 632	d 252 e 6.7	270 7.7
Saxby	a b c	6420 £426 -	10956 £617 6	12819 £724 13	11684 £1276 20	d 178 e 1.4	173 1.3
Edmondthorpe & Wymondham	a b c	not open	6262* £298* 0*	8618 £490 5	7090 £660 16	d 36 e 4.6	36 3.8
Whissendine	a b c	2984 £148 -	5691 £432 0	5603 £460 8	5556 £652 11	d 124 e 0.9	82 1.3
Ashwell	a b c	7288 £594 -	9891 £828 3	11108 £954 1	10538 £1206 17	d 142 e 1.5	102 2.0
Oakham	a b c	31276 £3516 -	37636 £4466 7	44866 £6041 12	44822 £9359 86	d 160 e 5.4	134 6.4
Manton	a b c	13766 £1302 -	16832 £1924 4	18899 £2431 11	20740 £4783 62	d 187 e 1.9	147 2.7
Luffenham	a b c	18683 £937 -	15152 £772 11	15176 £992 17	16925 £1882 52	d 82 e 3.6	75 4.3
Ketton & Collyweston	a b c	18483 £662 -	21715 £833 19	22430 £1004 23	25332 £1746 55	d 82 e 5.3	75 6.5

* year 1895 only (station opened 1894)

SECTION 4
LEICESTER & HITCHIN RAILWAY

		a passengers booked				d weekly train departures		
		b passenger receipts (incl. season tickets)				**e** average booked passengers boarding each train (excluding season ticket holders)		
		c season tickets						
		(annual averages from 3-year periods)						
		1872-4	1888-90	1905-7	1920-2		1905-7	1920-2
Wigston Magna	a	22161	65883	55716	53577	d	142	118
	b	£757	£2893	£2354	£3300	e	7.5	8.7
	c	-	347	170	196			
Great Glen	a	10423	12674	25814	24178	d	142	124
	b	£515	£663	£1549	£3116	e	3.5	3.7
	c	-	10	40	191			
Kibworth	a	29033	28733	39567	41014	d	142	124
	b	£2279	£2377	£3730	£7088	e	5.4	6.4
	c	-	26	111	296			
East Langton	a	7212 *	8716	12253	12256	d	124	112
	b	£371 *	£469	£818	£1400	e	1.9	2.1
	c	-	7	18	36			

SECTION 5
DERBY & ASHBY BRANCH AND SAWLEY & WESTON LINE

		1872-4	1888-90	1905-7	1920-2		1905-7	1920-2
Tonge & Breedon	a	3016	5192	5955	5711	d	74	63
	b	£126	£245	£337	£762	e	1.5	1.7
	c	-	2	5	18			
Worthington	a	7209	6606	8134	6606	d	73	63
	b	£391	£359	£399	£359	e	2.1	2.0
	c	-	0	10	0			
Castle Donington & Shardlow	a	22930	27523	32999	26058	d	200	136
	b	£1026	£1443	£1924	£3028	e	3.2	3.6
	c	-	11	44	132			

SECTION 6
NOTTINGHAM & MELTON LINE

		1872-4	1888-90	1905-7	1920-2		1905-7	1920-2
Old Dalby	a	7553**	7723	8139	8833	d	74	99
	b	£423**	£473	£492	£999	e	2.1	1.7
	c	-	4	8	37			
Grimston	a	5398**	6903	7322	7020	d	74	93
	b	£260**	£374	£376	£708	e	1.9	1.5
	c	-	7	4	24			

* 1877-9 instead of 1872-4 (station opened 1876)
** 1881-3 instead of 1872-4 (station opened 1880)

SECTION 9
ASHBY & NUNEATON JOINT RAILWAY (Midland Railway trains only)

	a	passengers booked			
	b	passenger receipts (incl. season tickets)			
	c	season tickets			
	(annual averages from 3-year periods)				
		1876-8	1888-90	1905-7	1920-2
Donisthorpe	a	7422	6759	4607	4827
	b	£197	£193	£170	£290
	c	-	0	7	62
Measham	a.	18907	9119	5590	6449
	b	£444	£414	£272	£668
	c	-	0	10	32
Snarestone	a	2524	1688	1398	2201
	b	£145	£120	£114	£272
	c	-	0	5	17
Shackerstone	a	7329	1750	2070	1361
	b	£240	£180	£163	£211
	c	-	0	0	15
Heather & Ibstock	a	3089	2572	10097	373
	b	£130	£151	£728	£96
	c	-	0	13	36
Hugglescote	a	3720	3349	7966	19
	b	£63	£34	£287	£9
	c	-	0	3	2
Market Bosworth	a	6356	2073	1913	1182
	b	£285	£181	£160	£304
	c	-	0	2	30
Shenton	a	697	603	572	400
	b	£37	£45	£32	£60
	c	-	1	0	6
Stoke Golding	a	1212	863	1052	1207
	b	£52	£56	£52	£80
	c	-	0	1	5
Higham-on-the Hill	a	1093	1036	992	967
	b	£32	£43	£28	£41
	c	-	0	1	1

SECTION 11
GREAT NORTHERN AND LONDON & NORTH WESTERN JOINT RAILWAY

		a	passengers booked			
		b	passenger receipts			
		c	season tickets			
		d	season ticket receipts			
		(annual av'ges from 3-yr periods)				**parcel receipts (annual av'ge from 1927-8)**
			1923-5* (LNER)	1936-8* (LNER)	1936-8* (LMS)	
Redmile		a	5219	1107	468	
		b	£377	£117	£32	£246
		c	NA	-	16	
		d	£8	-	£32	
Harby & Stathern		a	11192	1511	2211	
		b	£944	£240	£119	£803
		c	NA	-	75	
		d	£24	-	£54	
Long Clawson & Hose		a	2929	370	1557	
		b	£287	£56	£44	£558
		c	NA	-	9	
		d	£17	-	£6	
Scalford		a	3177	874	2580	
		b	£300	£131	£61	£781
		c	NA	7	14	
		d	£13	£19	£7	
Melton Mowbray North		a	12287	5356	5748	
		b	£2431	£1479	£352	£2273
		c	NA	45	6	
		d	£4	£37	£6	
Great Dalby		a	NA	694	3666	
		b	NA	£75	£95	NA
		c	NA	-	1	
		d	NA	-	£1	
John O'Gaunt		a	NA	2112	2937	
		b	NA	£200	£258	NA
		c	NA	-	11	
		d	NA	-	£12	
Tilton		a	NA	287	1058	
		b	NA	£25	£100	NA
		c	NA	-	8	
		d	NA	-	£14	
East Norton		a	NA	136	1906	
		b	NA	£28	£214	NA
		c	NA	-	17	
		d	NA	-	£26	
Hallaton		a	NA	312	5570	
		b	NA	£35	£370	NA
		c	NA	-	17	
		d	NA	-	£14	

* with the Company Grouping in 1923, the GNR became a constituent of the LNER and the LNWR a constituent of the LMS (although the line's title remained GN and LNW Joint Railway). Separate figures continued to be recorded by each station for the LNER and LMS business, but only the LNER figures are available for the 1923-5 period.

NA not available

SECTION 12
TILTON TO LEICESTER RAILWAY

		a passengers booked		
		b passenger receipts		
		c season tickets		
		d season ticket receipts		
		(annual av'ges from 3-yr periods)		parcel receipts (annual av'ge from 1927-8)
		1923-5	1936-8	
Leicester Belgrave Road	a	60647	27198	
	b	£9325	£6657	£747
	c	NA	71	
	d	£482	£52	
Humberstone	a	29472	11695	
	b	£2167	£1186	£110
	c	NA	18	
	d	£24	£22	
Thurnby & Scraptoft	a	14692	2816	
	b	£265	£72	£133
	c	NA	50	
	d	£118	£11	
Ingarsby	a	9821	3691	
	b	£353	£165	£147
	c	NA	196	
	d	£65	£74	
Lowesby	a	10349	3574	
	b	£408	£199	£596
	c	NA	197	
	d	£73	£92	

NA not available

SECTION 13
GREAT CENTRAL RAILWAY

		(annual av'ges from 3-yr periods)		parcel receipts (annual av'ge from 1927-8)
a passengers booked				
b passenger receipts				
c season tickets				
d season ticket receipts				
		1923-5	1936-8	
Loughborough Central	a	267700	147613	£3553
	b	£18968	£16154	
	c	NA	1562	
	d	NA	£1078	
Quorn & Woodhouse	a	68861	12799	£406
	b	£2739	£792	
	c	NA	638	
	d	NA	£342	
Rothley	a	71834	19096	£262
	b	£2295	£912	
	c	NA	558	
	d	£2201	£423	
Belgrave & Birstall	a	23768	13987	£80
	b	£605	£559	
	c	NA	1352	
	d	£674	£488	
Leicester Central	a	409189	235796	£52309
	b	£61297	£54002	
	c	NA	2321	
	d	£3845	£2243	
Dean & Dawson*	a	122598	NA	-
	b	£42677	NA	
	c	-	NA	
	d	-	NA	
Whetstone	a	41437	8998**	£307
	b	£1535	£615**	
	c	NA	7**	
	d	£114	£5**	
Ashby Magna	a	24333	19628	£529
	b	£968	£970	
	c	NA	1063	
	d	£1079	£366	
Lutterworth	a	68255	34339	£1539
	b	£4153	£3043	
	c	NA	1001	
	d	NA	£567	

NA   not available
* Leicester travel agency (figures of other agencies not recorded)
**1935-6 average (1937-8 NA)

BIBLIOGRAPHY AND SOURCES

PRIMARY SOURCES

Daily and weekly newspapers held in the Leicestershire Record Office and in the Coalville, Hinckley, Loughborough, Market Harborough and Melton Mowbray libraries. Not all of the runs are complete.

Ashby Gazette	1876-1888
Coalville Times	1893 onwards
Hinckley News/Times	1861 onwards
Leicester Advertiser	1842-1986
Leicester Chronicle	1827-1979
Leicester Daily Post	1872-1921
Leicester Guardian	1857-1876
Leicester Herald	1827-1833
Leicester Journal	1828-1920
Leicester Mail	1911-1963
Leicester Mercury	1874 onwards
Leicester Pioneer	1902-1928
Leicestershire Mercury	1836-1864
Loughborough Advertiser	1868-1882
Loughborough Echo	1912 onwards
Loughborough Herald &	
North Leics Gazette	1880-1919
Loughborough Monitor	1859-1867
Loughborough Monitor & News/	
Monitor & Herald/Monitor	1894-1977
Market Harborough Advertiser/Mail	1869 onwards
Melton Mowbray Mercury	1881-1915
Melton Times	1887 onwards

Various Company Board and Committee Minute books held at the Public Record Office, Kew.

Ashby & Nuneaton Joint Committee	Rail 11
Charnwood Forest Railway Company	Rail 108
Great Central Railway	Rail 226
Great Northern Railway	Rail 236
Leicester & Swannington Railway	Rail 359
London Midland & Scottish Railway	Rail 418
London & North Eastern Railway	Rail 390
(Traffic returns)	Rail 393/18-24,
	Rail 398/1-16
London & North Western Railway	Rail 410
Midland Counties Railway	Rail 490
Midland Railway	Rail 491
(Traffic returns)	Rail 491/672-77

Timetables held at the Public Record Office	Rail 900-999

SECONDARY SOURCES

Aldworth,C. *The Nottingham & Melton Railway 1872-1990,* 1990

Allen,E. *The Midland Counties Railway Companion,* 1840

Anderson,P.H. *Forgotten Railways: The East Midlands,* 1973

Anderson,V.R. & Fox,G.K. *A Pictorial Record of LMS Architecture,* 1981

Anderson,V.R. & Fox,G.K. *A Pictorial Record of Midland Railway Architecture,* 1985

Barman,C. *An Introduction to Railway Architecture,* 1951

Biddle,G. *Victorian Stations,* 1973

Biddle,G. *The Railway Surveyors,* 1990

Biddle,G. & Spence,J. *The British Railway Station,* 1977

Binney,M. & Pearce,D. (eds). *Railway Architecture,* 1979

Bradshaw,G. *Bradshaw's Railway Guide,* editions 1839 to 1961

Clinker,C.R. *The Leicester & Swannington Railway,* 1977

Clinker,C.R. & Firth,J.M. *Register of Closed Passenger Stations and Goods Depots, 1830-1970,* 1971

Clinker,C.R. & Hadfield,C. *The Ashby de la Zouch Canal and its Railways,* 1978

Cooper,A., Leggott,P. & Sprenger,C. *The Melbourne Military Railway,* 1990

Franks,D.L. *Great Northern and London & North Western Joint Railway,* 1974

Franks,D.L. *The Ashby & Nuneaton Joint Railway,* 1975

Gough,J. 'Leicester (London Road) Station' (in *The Adaption of Change,* ed D.Williams, 1980)

Gough,J. *The Northampton & Harborough Line,* 1984

Gough,J. *The Midland Railway - A Chronology,* 1989

Greville,M.D. & Spence,J. *Closed Passenger Lines of Great Britain, 1827-1947,* 1974

Healy,J.M.C. *Great Central Memories,* 1987

Hendry,R.Preston & Hendry,R.Powell *An Historical Survey of Selected LMS Stations, Layouts and Illustrations* (2 vols), 1982 & 1986

Hoskins,W.G. & McKinley,R.A. (eds). *Leicestershire's railways* (in *A History of the County of Leicester* vol 3, 1955)

Kalla-Bishop,P.M. 'Melbourne Military Railway' (in *Locomotives at War,* 1980)

Knighton,D.J.U. *A History and Guide to Rothley a Great Central Country Station,* 1989

Leleux,R. *A Regional History of the Railways of Great Britain vol 9: The East Midlands,* 1976

Lloyd,D. & Insall,D. *Railway Station Architecture,* 1977

Marshall,J. *A Biographical Dictionary of Railway Engineers,* 1978

Railway Clearing House, *Handbook of Railway Stations*, 1889, 1904, 1912, 1923, 1938, 1957

Rhodes,J. *Bourne to Saxby*, 1989

Rhodes,J. *The Uppingham to Seaton Railway*, 1990

Stevens,P.A. 'The Ashby & Nuneaton Joint Railway and Shackerstone Station' (in *Shackerstone, Guide to Leicestershire's Steam Branch Line*, c1983)

Stevenson,P.S. (ed). *The Midland Counties Railway*, 1989

Traylen,A.R. *Railways in Rutland*, 1980

Wishaw,F. *The Railways of Great Britain and Ireland*, 1840

MAGAZINE AND JOURNAL ARTICLES

Clinker,C.R. 'The Leicester & Swannington Railway', *Railway World*, vol 14, April 1953

Hall,W.T. 'The Ashby & Nuneaton Branch of the LMSR', *Railway Magazine*,vol LXX, May 1932

Hopwood,H.L. 'The Great Northern and London & North Western Joint Railway', *Railway Magazine*, vol XLII, Dec 1918

Meik,H.H. 'The Great Northern and London & North Western Railways in Leicestershire', *The Railway & Travel Monthly*, vol 9, Sept 1914

Munns,R.T. 'Bygone Days on a Leicestershire Joint Line', *Railway Magazine*, vol 100, March 1954

Oxley,J.F. & Smith,D.R. 'The Nottingham-Kettering Line of the LMR', *Trains Illustrated*, vol 12, June 1959

Riley,R.C. 'The Leicester West Bridge Branch', *Railway World*, vol 24, November 1963

Stevens,P.A. 'The Midland Railway's Syston & Peterborough Branch, 1845-8', *Journal of the Railway & Canal Historical Society*, vol XIX, March 1973

Walker,C.P. & Banyard,P.H.V. 'Leicester's Belgrave Road Branch Lives Another Year', *Trains Illustrated*, vol 14, July 1961

Walker,C.P. 'The GN & LNW Joint Line through Leicestershire', *Railway World*, vol 24, September 1963

UNPUBLISHED WORKS

Bentley,K.A. *A Study of Seaton Station LNWR*, 1979 *

Helsey,M. *A History of the Charnwood Forest Railway*, MA dissertation, Loughborough University, 1985

Sanderson,A. *The Great Central in Leicester*, c1966 *

Stretton,C.E. *Railways of Leicestershire* (compilation of printed articles), c1904 *

* held in the Leicestershire Record Office